Truth and Knowledge

Prelude to a Philosophy of Freedom

Rudolf Steiner

Introduction by Ronald H. Brady

Translated by Ronald H. Brady, Rita Stebbing and Frederick Amrine

Additional Notes by Paul M. Allen

With a Bibliography of Ronald H. Brady by Frederick Amrine

CW 3

CONTENTS

How We Make Sense of the World

A Study in Rudolf Steiner's Epistemological Work

Ronald H. Brady

A Theory of Knowledge *(Erkenntnistheorie)* was central to Rudolf Steiner's thought. By a theory of knowledge, however, Steiner meant to indicate an approach closely related to what is now termed phenomenology and thus quite distinct from the usual import of epistemology. This volume was constructed to explain these points, and their effect on the various projects of scientific methodology, ethics, and aesthetics that come out of Steiner's writings.

Historical Background

Philosophy in Germany during the second half of the nineteenth century was broadly identified with the theory of knowledge *(Erkenntnistheorie).* Natural science had overwhelmed all resistance, and since science was now the repository of all firm knowledge, the study of the sciences seemed to many the only task left, whether this was carried out in the guise of scientific epistemology or experimental psychology. But if science were the mode of knowing, then epistemology could only be a justification of the natural sciences, and would implicitly maintain their naturalistic viewpoint – that is, it would assume that all objects of knowledge are to be known according to the manner in which external nature is known, and would take the science of the day to be methodologically correct. Thus, prior to all investigation, this epistemology will rest on assumptions that prefigure the nature of the object of knowledge, and for that matter, the nature of the knowing subject. The dogmatism of such a position could only be recommended by someone already convinced of its authenticity.

The assumption that all modes of being could be reduced to something analogous to objects of external nature was challenged in German philosophy at the turn of the century by two students of Franz Brentano: Rudolf Steiner and Edmund Husserl. Husserl is the better known figure, and his 1900 *Logical Investigations (Logische Untersuchungen)* begins the critique of naturalism known as phenomenology, developing an argument that the naturalistic experience of the world is but one of the guises in which being appears. The method of phenomenology, according to Husserl, provided a means to investigate these varieties of experience. A little earlier William James had developed his notion of "radical empiricism," which bears certain similarities to the work of Husserl and Steiner. James was actually in communication with the former, and there could have been a cross-fertilization of ideas, although James does not appear to recognize the role of intentionality.

Steiner had developed his own critique of naturalism a few years earlier in his study of Goethe's method: A *Theory of Knowledge Implicit in Goethe's World Conception (Grundlinien einer Erkenntnistheorie der Goetheschen Weltanschauung)*, 1886; his dissertation: *Truth and Knowledge (Wahrheit und Wissenschaft)*, 1892; and *The Philosophy of Freedom (Philosophie der Freiheit)*, 1894. These works did not produce a new name or terminology, but like Husserl's later attack, attempted to change the meaning of *Erkenntnistheorie*.

6

Historically one can view both figures as part of the development of German epistemological reflection that moves from Kant through Fichte, Schelling and Hegel. They also share a more immediate background. While there is no record that Husserl and Steiner ever met during their studies with Brentano in Vienna, it seems obvious that their philosophic concerns are related to those of Brentano, who must be given credit for focusing philosophic attention upon mental phenomena, and turning toward the act of thinking rather than the results. Both Husserl and Steiner share this turn. Husserl describes phenomenology as the study of consciousness through reflection, or the "self-awareness" *(Selbst-besinnung)* of cognitive life. The goal of Steiner's dissertation was to allow "consciousness to come to terms with itself," and his method, as described in the later *Philosophy of Freedom,* was "introspective *(seelische)* observation." Like Husserl, he found that such self-consciousness provided a means to investigate the dimensions of experience, extending knowledge beyond the limits of naturalism. Steiner had other sources, as a reading of his autobiography will testify, but his debt to Brentano may be estimated from his memoir on his old professor in *Riddles of the Soul (Von Seelenrätseln),* published in 1917.

The parallels that seem to exist between Husserl and Steiner, however, spring from a common starting point (their examination of mental or *intentional* activity) rather than the manner in which they develop their later thought. In that development they differ widely, although each continues toward an extensive critique of western modes of conceptualization.

Goethe's methodology determines the shape of Steiner's early epistemological work, but the poet never examined intentionality itself. I have chosen to begin with Steiner's doctoral dissertation, which he credited with demonstrating that his thought "rests upon its own foundation, and need not be derived from Goethe's world-view."

Truth and Knowledge (Wahrheit und Wissenschaft)

The dissertation was published when Steiner was thirty-one, but accepted for his degree a few years earlier. The dissertation director noted that it was not the "expected" production, but was of such an "unusual nature" that it could still be accepted. The dissertation, a "Prolegomena to the reconciliation of philosophic consciousness with itself," was so narrowly focused on the self-grasp of thinking in the central chapters that some readers may have difficulty finding the context of Steiner's sentences. Of course, the editor has the advantage of hindsight created by knowledge of *The Philosophy of Freedom,* where the continuous commentary on related and opposing views aids the reader to see how Steiner would respond to the various positions of his day. In the dissertation the problem is presented against a background of neo-Kantian thought, but without the running commentary of the later work, and the middle chapters preserve a sense of discovery that is missing in the masterly treatment of the later *Philosophy.* We begin therefore with the published version of the dissertation, the subtitle of which reads, "Prelude to a Philosophy of Freedom."

However radical a break Steiner meant to make with the thought of his day, he had to couch his argument in terms of that very thought, especially in a dissertation. The first sentence of the 1891 preface reads: "Present day philosophy suffers from an unhealthy faith in Kant." That faith will be criticized in chapter one, the development of epistemology since Kant in chapter two. Both chapters are structured by the problematic put forth in the earlier section titled "Preliminary Remarks." The section begins:

Epistemology is the scientific study of what all other sciences presuppose without examining it: cognition itself. It is thus a philosophical science, fundamental to all other sciences. Only through epistemology can we learn the value and significance of all insight gained through the other sciences. Thus it provides the foundation for all scientific effort. It is obvious that it can fulfill its proper function only by making no presuppositions itself, as far as this is possible, about man's faculty of knowledge. This much is generally accepted. Nevertheless, when the better-known systems of epistemology are more closely examined it becomes apparent that a whole series of presuppositions are made at the beginning, which cast doubt on the rest of the argument. It is striking that such hidden assumptions are usually made at the outset, when the fundamental problems of epistemology are formulated. But if the essential problems of a science are misstated, the right solution is unlikely to be forthcoming. The history of science shows that whole epochs have suffered from innumerable mistakes that can be traced to the simple fact that certain problems were wrongly formulated ... (p. 79)

The germ of Steiner's approach is already implicit in his remarks on the erroneous formulations of epistemology. Obviously, the premises with which we begin an examination should not be identical with the conclusions that result from that same investigation, or the process is circular. Thus, if the question is: "how can we know the world?" or "how does the act of cognition take place?" we cannot begin with the very "knowledge" that this investigation should justify, or we investigate no more than the logical implications of our presuppositions. Epistemology, Steiner concludes, cannot begin from any positive knowledge of the world, but must suspend all such "knowing" in order to examine the act of knowing itself. The point is simple, but almost always ignored, due to the seeming impossibility of carrying out such a task. How can we begin without some knowledge of the world? How can the question be formula ted without knowing the parameters that comprise the problem? But if we do begin from such "knowledge" our epistemology will necessarily validate present sciences, and deny the possibility of any other form of science.

Most modern approaches, for example, take their starting-point from the apparent distinction between the thinking subject and the world external to that subject, and thus formulate epistemology after a Cartesian or Neo-Kantian framework. In this formulation, which we may term after Kant the "transcendental" formulation, the basic question of epistemology becomes: "what is the relation of thinking to being?" or "what is the relation of subjective consciousness to external or objective reality?" These questions arise from the assumed separation of the two – that is, thinking attempts to know the world of objective reality, which world is itself totally independent of thinking. In such a formulation, however, we already know something of that world (such as its difference from thinking), and the problem is created by what we know – that is, the distance between the thinking and its object.

Against this Steiner will propose that since we cannot take the results of previous cognition for granted when we attempt to grasp cognition itself, another formulation of the problem is necessary. If we simply propose that knowledge is immanent in human consciousness (if it is not, then we are not speaking about anything), the basic question of epistemology could be simply: How? What is the act of knowing? Thus we face toward our own act of cognition, and the investigation turns on the *self-observation of thinking* – finding a way to watch what we do – rather than a presupposed knowledge of the world. This "immanent" position (termed "monistic" in *The Philosophy of Freedom*) will be presented in chapters four and five, but before it can be advanced, current forms of "transcendental" epistemology (termed "dualistic" 'in the *Philosophy*) must be rejected. ("Immanent" and "transcendent" are used in Steiner's early commentaries on Goethe's science.)

Having announced his problem, Steiner will spend the first three chapters clearing the field – showing that those formulations accepted in his day all begin from a presumed but questionable knowledge of the world.

Chapter one is titled, "Kant's Basic Epistemological Question," which question Steiner identifies as: "How are synthetic judgments possible *a priori?*" Synthetic judgments, according to Kant, are those through which the predicate adds something new to the object – as opposed to analytic judgments, in which the predicate simply makes explicit something already contained in the object. (For instance, "your deafness is caused by a torn eardrum" is a reasonable diagnosis for the doctor to make, and it is synthetic, since it connects something new to the fact of deafness. On the other hand, should the doctor say that "Your deafness is due to an impairment of your hearing," you would do well to ask for your money back, since by analytic judgment you know that deafness is an impairment of hearing, and the doctor is not telling anything more than "you are deaf because you are deaf." If the doctor is to be worth his fee, he must make a synthetic judgment, explaining the symptom by connecting something new to it – that is, a cause.)

Because David Hume had shown that a judgment of causal relation, a prime example of synthetic judgment, cannot rest on sensible evidence alone, Kant became interested in how synthetic judgments were made. He decided that they must derive from the action of the mind rather than the evidence of the senses. If the mind must add something to the evidence of the senses in order to formulate a causal judgment, he reasoned, this addition must have the form of a presupposition assumed prior to the evidence. Thus his question, when he sets about to investigate the process of cognition, becomes "how are synthetic judgments possible a priori" (prior to all experience).

Steiner spends the first chapter examining Kant's question, and argues that it is more conclusion than question. Given that a synthetic judgment differs from an analytic one through a different activity of the mind, and even allowing that here the mind appears to add something to the evidence of the senses, it still does not follow that this contribution must take the form of an *a priori* contribution. Since Kant has assumed that our categories are preformed in our faculty of judgment, he must also assume that experience can neither supply these categories nor support the same – that is, we add the categories due to our nature, not the nature of the experience we encounter. Steiner argues that at the outset it is unclear whether the mind fits all experience into *a priori* categories, or creates them in response to the determinations of experience.

Obviously a direct investigation of mental activity is in order, but Kant does not investigate this activity directly, preferring instead to work out a schematic of the structure of the mind on the assumption that the mind contains *a priori* categories. Thus Kant did not speak to the project of epistemology proposed by Steiner.

Steiner's second chapter is given to "Epistemology Since Kant," and deals mainly with the assumption that all our experience consists of "representations" *(Vorstellungen)* of reality rather than reality itself. Given the number of references in this chapter, it seems clear that the major epistemological discussion of his day was put forward within this framework. The line of reasoning, which is derivative from Kant, takes on a somewhat crude form in those given to scientific thought. The general argument in these quarters would run: The world as we immediately experience it seems to be the world of ultimate reality to the "naïve realist" (the individual who makes no question of his perceptions), when in actuality experience is but the form in which our senses represent that reality. Thus Steiner quotes Eduard von Hartmann summing up the position:

> The content of consciousness consists fundamentally of
> the sensations that are the soul's reflex response to
> processes of movement in the uppermost part of the
> brain, and these have not the slightest resemblance to
> the molecular movements that called them into being.
> (p. 87)

Although the term "soul" would no longer be used, forms of this argument still abound in experimental psychology and cognitive science. Steiner's complaint fits them just as well as it fit von Hartmann's version.

At stake in this account is the nature of the immediate experience. If we already know that the subject is so separated from the "real" objects that he or she does not perceive these "in themselves" but must construct "representations" of them, then it must follow that because the human perceiver has either added to or substituted for the actual objects, the representations cannot be identical to the originals. For those who begin from this "truth," as von Hartmann would have us do, the reality of the world is never apparent – we are always looking at our own creations and attempting to infer from these how the things-in-themselves were prior to our constructive activity.

Such lines of argument all begin from the established world-view of the natural sciences, and therefore from "knowledge" of perception and mind that is relatively advanced. In such accounts the nature of perception and the relation of consciousness to the external world are presumed known, for nature is already an object of scientific understanding. There are two objections to consider. The first and most important would be that such claims are already too rich for an epistemological starting point. Where is the presupposition of correct knowledge investigated? Where do we find a justification of the use of such notions as "brain," "molecular movements," and "representations"? How is it that we already know that the problem should be cast in these terms? Obviously, any account of cognition that was able to begin without dependence on these presumptions could easily bring them into question, and thus their weakness becomes apparent. Writers who begin here already know too much.

Secondly, were the origin of these presuppositions to be investigated it would seem that the line of argument is contradictory. We come by the brain and its representations of molecular movements by an investigation of the perceptual anatomy of the human being. This investigation takes some elements of immediate experience – that is, the brain and nerves – to be a correct picture of the world, yet it still calls the objects of experience "representations." One wants to object that they cannot have it both ways. Either the perceived objects are representations of reality rather than reality itself, or this is not the case, but we cannot suppose that the interactions of the brain and nerves, themselves but representations, create all representations including – of necessity – the brain and nerves.

Again, if at any point in the chain of perception a received impression "has not the slightest resemblance" to its source, then the naïve realism which supposes something to be real because it is perceived is called into question, and we certainly cannot begin an epistemology with these references. As any examination of epistemological positions will show, however, such presuppositions almost always begin the discussion. In the argument that follows, however, Steiner will depart from the tradition of epistemology since Kant by formulating the problem of cognition without any dependence upon an assumed knowledge of the world.

Or, for that matter, an assumed knowledge of cognition. One of the immediate signs that we are departing into new ground is the following discussion on naïveté of thinking:

> The subjectivism outlined above is based on *the use of thinking* for elaborating certain facts. This presupposes that, starting from certain facts, a correct conclusion can be obtained through logical thinking (logical combination of particular observations). But the *justification* for using thinking in this way is not examined by this philosophical approach. This is its weakness. While naïve realism begins by assuming that the content of perceptual experience has objective reality without examining if this is so, the standpoint just characterized sets out from the equally uncritical conviction that thinking can be used to arrive at scientifically valid conclusions. In contrast to naive realism, this view could be called naïve rationalism (p. 89)

Such naïveté, Steiner argues, can be overcome only by a grasp of the laws inherent in the operations of cognition, a knowledge that he obviously does not find in the epistemology of his day. The chapter concludes:

> Epistemology can only be a critical science. Its object is an eminently subjective activity of man: cognition, and it seeks to demonstrate the laws inherent in cognition. Thus all naïveté must be excluded from this science. Its strength must lie in doing precisely what many thinkers, inclined more toward practical action, pride themselves that they have never done: namely, "thinking about thinking." (p. 89)

(The last phrase is a Goethe reference, since the poet once remarked that he had been clever, and avoided "thinking about thinking." Steiner's use of the quote here performs a double duty. Given his admiration for Goethe's work, it assures the reader of the possible worth of naïve effort. But it also severs the present work from any dependence on Goethe, a point that Steiner mentioned in his preface.)

In the next chapter Steiner will begin an examination of the operations of cognition that attempts to avoid all forms of naïveté. Readers already familiar with Husserl may, in the following section, find the contrast between the philosophers quite surprising, for Husserl's approach has naturally defined the problem for them and Steiner may seem to bear no resemblance at all. But of course Steiner cannot make use of the specialized terminology developed in Husserl's later efforts. He lays down his own road, and the reader must make the same journey to understand his conclusion. Reference to a second framework - that is, Husserl - will become instructive only after each is approached independently.

The Starting Point of Epistemology

This chapter returns to the notion of a "starting point," with the intention of providing one that does not presuppose what it cannot defend. That the premises of most contemporary *Erkenntnistheorie* cannot be defended has been his point so far, and of course, since critique can hardly fault a subtraction of premises, it would seem that Steiner's preliminary tactic is self-justifying. But the real target of Steiner's criticism may not be visible to the reader until his proposed "starting point" is worked through.

It would appear, for example, that we generate thought in order to apply it to the phenomena of our experience, which appearances meet us prior to thought. The assumption that thought is an element added to the phenomenal world – in an effort to create an ideal replication – is ubiquitous in most fields, and leads to a demand that epistemology provide criteria by which to judge the accuracy of the replication. Thus the *problem of knowledge* is created by the assurance that thought is *in here,* reflecting or replicating a world *out there,* and this is the "knowledge" that Steiner is actually discarding, although the candid reader will notice that it is so ingrained in our mental habits as to seem almost undiscardable.

A few notes before we read the chapter. The term most often translated by "cognition" is *erkennen,* which can be translated as knowing, recognizing, perceiving, apprehending, discerning, distinguishing. The noun *Erkenntnis* is best translated as knowledge or understanding. Thus the movement of mind toward comprehension is the basic indication, and I have used *cognition* in this general sense. By *knowledge* and *cognition* Steiner means the accurate grasp of some reality in the world, so the *problem of knowledge* deals with knowledge of the world – not with a grasp of our own thought, which grasp Steiner takes to be unproblematic. This is a fundamental point in his argument. Just because we can grasp our own acts of meaning (or our own intentions, in the language of phenomenology), Steiner contends, it is possible to reconstruct the way our knowledge of the world actually comes about – that is, the way the mind "wakes up" to the world. But this investigation of how our own mental activity creates knowledge cannot be formulated as an engineering problem, for it is not based on a relation between naturalistic objects.

Most readers are quite familiar with naturalistic formulations. For example, we ask: given a physical world, how does the physical human being come to understand it? – or given the impulses of the senses, how do we come to understand their source? – or given our representations, how can we infer the reality behind them? ... etc. We might call this the "problem solving" formulation since that mode of thought begins from known and therefore determinate entities, and investigates what follows from these determinations.

Upon reflection, this is the sort of description a third party might make of our cognition, as long as this being was not describing its own form of cognition. After all, the problem-solving approach takes its own knowledge of the parameters of the problem for granted. When one cannot do this however, when by the *problem of knowledge* we mean to address the problem of our own knowing, we cannot do this from outside.

Thus the investigation of our own cognition, *for us,* cannot begin with what is already known about the world, for that begs the question. Instead of beginning with what we "know" of the world, a theory of cognition must discover what *knowing* is: how our cognitive activity comes to know anything in the first place. We already appear to understand something of the world, but we can comprehend this understanding only by thinking back along the paths by which it came to be. Obviously, if we do not know how our cognition was formed, we do not know its value.

Can the problem be investigated in this manner? As Steiner suggested in his "Preliminary Remarks" quoted above, an inquiry is useful only to the degree that its question is properly formulated. But since his own formulation will discard presuppositions normally taken as integral to the problem, one of the first questions that will occur to his readers is whether, after subtracting so much, he can still define a problem. This is a useful response. Let me explain.

Consider how there can be a problem of knowledge at all, and what elements must be retained to retain the problem. At this junction we should notice that implicit within all forms of epistemology is the assurance that (1) we have a grasp of our own thinking – that is, we know what we mean, and (2) when our thinking activity begins, it does not do so in a vacuum, but responds to something other than itself, to something *given* that our thinking attempts to grasp. (Recall that in Steiner's text *knowledge* and *cognition* always refer to a grasp of the *other-than-thinking .)* There is a *problem* of knowledge just because we are unclear about how thinking can comprehend the *other,* and this recognition of the *other-than-thinking* is fundamental, although often in a confused form.

I say "confused" because we are usually very unclear about how this recognition came about, and due to this many unjustified assumptions are usually attached to the basic insight. We rarely comprehend, for example, that only our own cognitive activity and something *other* than that activity are necessary to structure the problem. Instead, usual habits of thought suppose that if we know *that* something other than thinking is given to thinking we must possess some grasp of *what* this other may be. But the two relations are different, and the second is not contained in the first.

After all, there could be no problem for cognition if another was not given to it, but there would still be nothing for cognition to do if the *what* of the other were also given rather than left for cognition to determine. Thus the naive insistence that there must be something "out there" confuses our assurance that we must be dealing with another with an assumption of what the other must be – the "out there," representing the mode of understanding applied to external objects in the world characterized by "common sense." But as we see, this naturalism is not basic to the problem any more than the mere impression that there is an *other-than-thinking* can specify what kind of *other* it may be. (Once we come to see clearly how this impression of an *other-than-thinking* is actually given to us, we could discard any tendency to suppose that the *what* must be given with it, but that step can only be taken later, when our orientation permits us to do so.)

Steiner's epistemological argument will occupy two chapters. Chapter four, which seeks the "departure point" for a theory of knowledge, advances by reconstructing intelligible recognition, or in the ordinary meaning of the term, *perception.* The chapter is divided in two "steps."

The first seeks for determining factors that we may take as original – that is, factors that will create and structure the problem. Steiner does this by reconstructing the act of knowing, beginning with those conditions actually *given* to the cognitive act *as it begins.* Obviously these conditions are crucial, for our activity will respond to them. But this simple question immediately puts the investigation on unusual ground. The first act of cognition appears to be recognition, even if this were only a recognition that *something was given,* but the conditions that meet our cognitive activity as it begins must lie prior to any recognition – or understanding – of the same. We can describe such conditions only by negation: by identifying and subtracting all those relations supplied by a recognition of the given. The result will be merely formal; the given just before thinking becomes active is utterly beyond any positive predication. It is everything that can be directly given without any relations yet established, thus for us everything is as yet unrecognized, and therefore unknown.

This firmly negative conclusion forces a new formulation of epistemology: as cognition begins, its first task is how to establish relations within a field (the given) where they are completely absent. Thus no reference to our subsequent "knowledge" of the world can be of any service here. These references would not be available, for us, when we face the virgin field of the given untouched by our activity.

If the field is without enough determination to define what cognition shall do with it, we are forced to turn in a new direction. After all, our sense that the task" could not follow from the nature of the *other-than-thinking,* which is indeterminate, but *by the teleology of thinking itself.* By direct examination of our own intentions in thinking we see that our effort to think demands an intelligible object of thinking: when we intend to think, we mean to take hold of something that is transparent to our activity. Actually, it is only this demand, made by our own cognitive activity, which now remains to define a problem. From it, we may determine that we must find a point in the given which is transparent to thinking if we are to recognize it at all.

Thus, due to the impossibility of deriving a determination from anything else, Steiner turns to the discovery of "intentional activity" as it will be called in phenomenology, and then allows this activity to postulate a starting point within the collective reference of "the given." This starting point, however, cannot be further outlined in these notes but must be worked through.

The examination begins:

> As we have seen in the preceding chapters, an
> epistemological investigation must begin by
> rejecting existing knowledge. Knowledge is
> something brought into existence by the human
> being -something that has arisen through human
> activity. If a theory of knowledge is really to
> explain the whole sphere of knowledge then it
> must start from something still quite untouched
> by the activity of thinking, and moreover,
> something that lends to this activity its first
> impulse. This starting point must lie outside the
> act of cognition, it must not itself be knowledge.
> But it must be sought immediately prior to
> cognition, so that the very next step the knower
> takes beyond it is the act of cognition. This
> absolute starting point must be determined in
> such a way that it admits nothing already derived
> from the act of knowing. (p. 90)

Notice that this starting point – outside cognition and
therefore not knowledge – removes any resemblance between
Steiner's effort and the usual formulations of the problem of
knowledge, based, as they are, on an assumed knowledge of the
world. Even so, the fundamental outline of all epistemological
formulations is already present; that is, given an *other than
thinking,*"how do we come to grasp it by thinking? But where the
usual *formulations* depend upon reference to some sort of
determinate structure in the given, Steiner takes another turn.

Only our immediately given world-image *(Weltbild)* can offer such a starting point, that is, that which lies before us prior to subjecting it to the process of cognition in any way, before we have asserted or decided anything about it by means of thinking. This "directly given" is what passes us by, and what we pass by, disconnected but still not divided into individual "entities, in which nothing appears distinguished from, related to, or determined by anything else … Before our conceptual activity begins, the world-picture contains neither substance, quality, nor cause and effect; distinction between matter and spirit, body and soul, do not yet exist. Furthermore any other predicates must be excluded at this stage. The picture can be considered neither as reality nor as appearance, neither subjective nor objective, neither as chance nor as necessity; whether it is a "thing-in-itself" or mere representation cannot be decided at this stage. As we have seen, a knowledge of physics or physiology which leads to a classification of the "given" under one or the other of the above headings cannot be the basis for a theory of knowledge. (p. 90)

The rhetorical difficulty of the passage turns on the problem created by negations. The "not known" must be that which is not grasped by the marks of what is knowable – that is, intelligible. It is neither "here," nor "not here," but "passes by," which character-ization cannot be taken as a positive state. It is not connected, but contrary to the apparent implication, it is not divided. While it is called a world-image or picture, it would seem to picture nothing if nothing within it is distinguished from anything else. The resulting referent lies beyond all positive assertions – all predicates.

Why describe by negation? Since we are speaking of our own cognition – of how the situation must be *for us* as we begin to think rather than for a third person who already knows – the strategy is a necessary one. Prior to any recognition on our part, the world cannot already possess, *for us,* what it will gain through that recognition. The description by negation is a way of identifying and subtracting all that belongs to cognition. This process removes all characterizations from the precognitive given except that it is *given* prior to cognition, and this is present to our first activity.

Of course, despite this very plain denial that any positive characterization can be advanced toward the given, a reader's search for an experiential example may produce an attempt to read the antecedent *given* as something recognizable. After all, we appear to experience the objects of our phenomenal world first and think about them second. If we accept this, then the given appearances are not without the listed qualities – that is, they are divided into individual entities, interrelated (spatially), mutually determined, constituting a clear image, etc. – all the qualities that we will recognize in the appearances after we have begun to think. But if this reading is an understandable mistake, it is still mistaken.

If the phenomenal world, with all its immediate intelligibility, appears to us without our cognitive effort, what need is there for such effort at all? What will recognition add? Presumably understanding – but the individual who clearly sees multiple objects in the room already understands that there are multiple objects in the room. Again we run afoul of the logical necessity that the conditions that meet us before we recognize must be distinguishable from those that result from our recognition. What is the room like, *for us,* before we have grasped anything at all? Here we can find no relation to experience. The room exists, *for us,* only when we have *noticed* that it does.

Thus we may approach from another angle. Although we cannot speak of what the world is like before we have understood anything, we can speak of what a scene is like before we have had any recognition of a particular object in the scene. When a friend points out the object we are startled by a sudden recognition and exclaim, "Oh, but I never noticed it!" Of course, to "notice" in this example is to recognize, and implies a mental act by which we become conscious of an object. Thus we find again that any solution which models mental activity as an addition that simply replicates what is already apparent is not satisfactory as an analysis.

Nor is it a possible reading of the text. Returning to the above description, we see that the claim was not that nothing was thought about as distinguished from anything else, but nothing "appears distinguished." In a footnote to the last sentence above Steiner adds: "Differentiation of the undifferentiated given into individual entities is already a result of cognitive activity." The grammar is clear – it is the *given* that is said to be undifferentiated, and which must await cognitive activity in order to gain differentiation. Thus reference is not to thoughts about appearances but to the condition of appearances. The "immediately given *Weltbild"* cannot yet contain the relations by which we pick out individual entities or differentiate them (remember that unity is also a relation), and thus cannot be identical with the phenomenal world.

Since his original "given" is not the phenomenal world, Steiner immediately cautions the reader that he or she will not find it in experience.

> If a being with a fully developed human intelligence were suddenly created out of nothing and then confronted with the world, the first impression on his senses and his thinking would be something like what I have just characterized as the unmediated given. In practice, we never encounter the given in this form – that is, there is never an experienced division between a pure, passive turning toward the given and the cognitive grasp of the given. (p. 90)

We cannot experience such a state, nor could anyone else, for Steiner's thought experiment of sudden creation is advanced only to emphasize the point that "in practice ... there is never an experienced division" between the *given* and the cognitive grasp of the same. Because this is the case, Steiner recognizes that objections are bound to be raised, such as Eduard von Hartmann's argument that since we are not beings who perceive the world *de nova* but have a history, we must start from the world apparent to the consciousness of the investigator (in this case, a philosopher). But as we saw above, von Hartmann uses this argument to defend an acceptance of much of modern science. The argument confounds the obvious truth that we must start where we are with the obvious fallacy that the past conclusions embedded in "where we are" must be true. What von Hartmann offers is a sophisticated attempt to defend the "in here" versus "out there" structure of a problem-solving approach.

But since the whole point of his approach is to avoid this fallacy, Steiner will demand a method by which we may eliminate any "predicates mediated through cognition." Such predicates, he writes, "cannot be accepted uncritically but must be carefully removed from the unmediated given so that it can be considered free of anything produced through the process of cognition."

> The division between the "given" and the "known" will not in fact coincide with any stage of human development; the boundary must be drawn artificially. But this can be done at every level of development so long as we draw the dividing line correctly between what confronts us free of all cognitive determinations, and what cognition subsequently makes of it. (p. 91)

Mindful of the objection that he has already used "a number of conceptual definitions," Steiner adds:

> what we have extracted by means of thought does not characterize the directly given, nor define or express anything about it; what it does is to guide our attention to the dividing line where the starting point of cognition is to be found ... To remove ... all that has been contributed by cognition, and to establish a precognitive starting point, can only be done conceptually. But such concepts are not of value as knowledge; they have the purely negative function of removing from sight all that belongs to knowledge and of leading us to the point where knowledge begins. These considerations act as signposts pointing to where cognition first appears, but at this stage do not themselves form part of the act of cognition. (p. 91)

But notice that to negate "all that belongs to knowledge " we must have a notion of what knowledge is, and the investigation is obviously guided by our grasp of our own knowing. This is even more obviously the case in the next passage, where Steiner reformulates the Aristotelian argument that all error is cognitive in nature, and concludes that error can begin only as the cognitive process begins. The precognitive given does not contain errors (there are no errors of sense).

> All error is also excluded from this starting point, for error can begin only with cognition, and therefore cannot arise before cognition sets in.
>
> Only a theory of knowledge that starts from considerations of this kind can claim to observe this last principle. If the starting point is some object (or subject) to which a conceptual determination is attached, then the possibility of error is already present in the starting point, namely the determination itself. Justification of the determination will depend upon the laws inherent in the act of cognition but these laws can be discovered only in the course of the investigation. Error is only excluded when one says: I remove from my world-picture all determinations arrived at through cognition and retain only what enters the horizon of my observation without activity on my part. When on principle I make no claim I also make no mistake.
>
> Error, in relation to knowledge, can occur only within the act of cognition. Sense deceptions are not errors. That the moon upon rising appears larger than it does at its zenith is not an error but a fact governed by the laws of nature. A mistake in knowledge would occur only if, in using thinking to combine the given perceptions, we interpret this "larger" and "smaller" in a

correct manner. This interpretation, however, lies within the act of cognition. (p. 92)

(We should note, before commenting on the substance of this last argument, that it is a reply to a specific complaint – that is, that illusions are due to the senses – and therefore is cast on the conceptual level assumed by the complaint. Of course, to see the moon at all, and differentiate it from other objects so that it may seem, in terms of its contrast with those objects, "larger" than usual, is, in terms of Steiner's analysis, already a complex cognitive act. But he points only at the appellation of error.)

The correction to the usual notion of "optical illusions" reveals a cognitive act where the popular notion of a "deception of the senses" misses it. Sense appearances are often said to be deceptive, but since they merely present and do not interpret, they cannot in themselves be erroneous. The case in point is that the moon looks larger on the horizon. This observation could only be mistaken if the moon did not in fact look larger on the horizon. I am mistaken, however, if I suppose that measurements, let us say in degrees of arc, of the width of the two appearances of the moon (on the horizon and at zenith) will show a discrepancy. Under certain conditions an optical distance or width will accurately foretell the measurements of the same. Under the conditions met in what is termed "optical illusion" this coordination between optical impression and measurement is lost. But such a situation represents an "illusion" – a mistake – only for the individual judge's measurement by optical impression. His unrealistic expectations arise from the judgment he has made. They are no more an error of sense than the apparent bending of a stick that extends through the surface of water. I must add a false cognitive judgment – such as, the stick will be bent when I take it out of the water – to constitute an error. The *look* of something cannot be mistaken because it makes no judgment, but the judgment by which we connect further expectations to that appearance can easily err.

Moving on, Steiner now takes a final argumentative step in his rejection of the naturalistic formulation of epistemology, showing that the very categories that structure it – subject and object, consciousness and external world – are the products of thinking and cannot constitute a prior framework. The argument runs as follows.

Since before cognition begins the given field is *given* but not yet *understood,* the field contains only that which may be directly given – directly presented in some sense of the term. The relations inherent in the field are not apparent, for they wait upon the cognitive act to become so. (Of course, if all relations are missing, even "larger" and "smaller," or difference in general, will not be present, and the field will not possess a "look.") To gain a sense of what might be present in this field we may compile a list of what might be identified after the fact of cognition. With a nod to von Hartmann's objection that the philosopher must begin where he or she is, Steiner suggests that everything we normally suppose to be found in consciousness can be included in the list, as long as we understand that as yet we have no judgments – no predications and thus no errors – attached to the list or to consciousness. (Such a list could only be compiled after the fact of cognition, but Steiner is demonstrating that even if we were correct in assuming that all these things were present, the usual structure of the problem would still not apply.

> This directly given content includes everything that enters our experience in the widest sense: sensations, perceptions, opinion, feelings, deeds, pictures of dreams and imaginations, representations, concepts and ideas.

Illusions and hallucinations too, at this stage are
equal to the rest of the given, for their other perceptions
can be revealed only through observation based on
cognition. (p. 92)

Illusions and hallucinations cannot yet be known to be such –
"are equal to the rest of the given" – because their relation to other
contents of the given can only be known "though observation based on
thinking." But once such a list is advanced, something less obvious
emerges.

When epistemology starts from the assumption that all
the elements just mentioned constitute the content of
our consciousness, the following question immediately
arises: How is it possible for us to go beyond our
consciousness and recognize actual existence; where
can the leap be made from subjectivity to the
transsubjective?
When such an assumption is not made, the
situation is different. Both consciousness and the
representation of the "I" are, to begin with only parts
of the directly given and the relationship of the latter to
the two former must be discovered by means of
cognition. Cognition is not to be defined in terms of
consciousness, but vice versa: *both consciousness and
the relation between subject and object in terms of
cognition.* Since the "given" is originally without
predicates, the question becomes how can it be
determined at all: how can any start be made with
cognition? (p. 93 – italics mine)

In the second of these last two paragraphs Steiner reformulates the problem of knowledge from a "transcendental" frame to an "immanent" one. The first paragraph proceeds from the assumption that all such elements are to be found only within subjective consciousness, which assumption generates the problem of how we will pass beyond this consciousness and all its contents to that externality (the transsubjective"): a problem which we all recognize. But *subjective* is "a predicate mediated by cognition," and the *in here* and *out there* of consciousness and externality is not simply given: it is a relation, and as such, must be discovered by cognition. The inner-outer relation of subject and object is just not there before cognition, and thus it cannot be used to frame the situation when we begin to think, being itself a product of that thinking.

If no relations have been determined, and we have only the contents of the given field to work with, the first question for us cannot be "how can we move from the subjective to the transsubjective?" (w have not yet recognized these two categories) but how can we reach *any* determinations, including "subjective" and "transsubjective"? Stating this conclusion in a more direct manner, our problem becomes how to identify and relate the contents of the given field. (The "given field" may be identified as the "field of consciousness," but since at this point consciousness cannot be supposed subjective, it is just the field in which the given is presented for thinking.)

Readers of William James will notice a similarity to his "methodological postulate" of a "pure experience," which experience would be prior to any conceptual relations, including internal-external or subject-object. Unfortunately James's inattention to the intentional function left him without a means to investigate the activity of cognition. Thus he never fully eliminates the popular prejudice that what is given before cognition is somehow more "concrete" than what cognition makes of it, a task which Steiner will complete in the next chapter.

Evidently any and all grounds for understanding the structure of the world can arise only from our operations with regard to this given field. Thus cognition can do nothing else but make its start from the field *as it is given.* Cognition must respond to a content that is, *for cognition,* totally indeterminate.

With this argument the first step draws to a close, and we should pause for reflection. At this junction the reader may feel that the above conclusion makes the problem impossible – if the *given* is indeterminate it may as well not be given; all we can do now is invent a world out of our own thinking. But that was the Kantian reaction, and it reveals hidden premises that must now be made to surface.

Let us examine our reaction more carefully. The impression that this task is impossible arises through the comparison of an undetermined given with our sense that thinking takes hold of the other through its intelligible determinations. Daily experience seems to illustrate this – after all, we grasp the world through determinations that are plainly "there" for our grasp. As I remarked above, when we think, we intend an object of thought that is transparent (intelligible) to our thinking. But if no such object is presented to us prior to our own act, how will that act find anything to grasp? How can cognition make any start without an intelligible object with which to begin? It is this response that sets up the question of step two: can cognition make a start without determinate phenomena? That it must and can do so is the demonstration of the second step.

We must find the bridge from the world as given to the world-picture that we build up through cognition. Here however, we meet with the following difficulty: As long as we merely stare passively at the given we will never find a point of attack where we can gain a foothold, and from where we can proceed with cognition. Somewhere in the given we must find a place where we can set to work ... (p. 93)

Our thinking, as noted above, usually proceeds by its grasp of determinations, and this would suggest that something determinate must be given to it if it is to respond. Such an expectation, however, arises from a grasp of the nature of thinking rather than any knowledge of the *other-than-thinking,* and here Steiner completes his turn from the usual starting point – the assumed nature of the world – to the *self-grasp of thinking,* and thus to what I have termed the discovery of intentionality.

Somewhere in the given we must find a place where we can set to work, where something exists which is akin to cognition ... real cognition depends on finding a sphere somewhere in the given where our cognizing activity does not merely presuppose something given, but finds itself active in the very essence of the given. In other words, precisely through strict adherence to the given as merely given it must become apparent that not everything in the given fits this description. The prerequisite we set up must be such that through strict adherence it cancels itself. We set it up not to pose an arbitrary starting point but to find the actual one. The given, in our sense of the term, can include that which in its most inward nature is not-given. The latter would appear, to begin with, as *formally* part of the given, but

on closer scrutiny would reveal its own nature out of
itself. (p. 93)

The qualification above that "real cognition depends on finding a
sphere somewhere in the given where our cognizing activity ... finds
itself active in the very essence of the given" is now quite recognizable.
It was the basis of the expectation of intelligible objects mentioned
above. That the given lacks determinations is not problematic in itself,
but this situation represents a difficulty when we attempt *to know* the
given. When we assume this purpose (knowing) we have an idea of
our goal, namely an object of thought which is transparent to
thought; something "akin to cognition," or directly intelligible. But
consider what makes thought directly intelligible to our gaze.

> The whole difficulty in understanding cognition
> comes from the fact that we ourselves do not create
> the content of the world. If we did this, cognition
> would not exist at all. I can only ask questions about
> something which is given to me. Something that I
> create myself I also determine myself, so that I need
> not ask for an explanation of it. (p. 93)

In the language of phenomenology what we "intend" (in the
specific sense to be explained in the next chapter) is transparently
clear to us, which is very close to *knowing what we mean.* It is just the
clear understanding that ideas arise out of our own activity that
makes us worry about whether they are just our own conventions or
carry "transsubjective" applicability. In the present context, however,
we do not have that particular problem, and the fact that our ideas

are clear to us because we determine or *mean* them can now be used to define the felt problem.

> Real cognition depends on finding a sphere
> somewhere in the given where our cognizing activity
> does not merely presuppose something given, but
> finds itself active in the very essence of the given ...
> This is the second step in our theory of knowledge. It
> consists in the postulate: In the sphere of the given
> there must be something in relation to which our
> activity does not hover in emptiness, but where the
> content of the world itself enters this activity. (p. 93)

The discussion that follows introduces a new consideration:

> Just as we specified that the starting point of a theory of
> knowledge must precede all cognition so that
> preconceptions could not cloud our cognitive activity,
> so now we specify the next step so that there can be no
> question of error or incorrect judgment. For this step
> prejudges nothing, but simply specifies what conditions
> must obtain if knowledge is to arise at all. It is essential
> that through critical reflection we become fully
> conscious of the fact that it is we who postulate what
> characteristic feature must be possessed by that part of
> the world-content with which our cognitive activity can
> make a start.

This, in fact, is the only thing we can do. The world-content as given is completely undetermined. No part of it of its own accord can provide the occasion for setting it up as the starting point to bring order out of chaos. The activity of thinking must therefore issue a decree and declare what characteristics such a part must manifest. Such a decree in no way infringes upon the qualities of the given. It does not introduce any arbitrary assumptions into epistemology. In fact, it asserts nothing about the given at all, but states only that if knowledge is to be explained, then we must look for some point in the given that has the characteristics described above. If such a region can be found, cognition can be explained, but not otherwise. Thus, while the given provides a general starting point for our account, our focus must now be narrowed to this particular point. (p. 94)

Of course, since the "postulate" follows from the nature of thinking and not that of the given, this demand is one that we give to ourselves. The activity of thinking can grasp only that which is like itself – that is, determined or meant by our own activity. But in this phrasing the notion that thinking "finds itself active in the very essence of the given" becomes "where the content of the world itself enters this activity – where the world is intelligible because it is *meant by us.* (See the discussion of intentionality in the next section.) ·

Following this intuited teleology we can sort out the list of possible given contents above.

Where, within the given, do we find something

that is not merely given, but only given insofar as it is brought forth in the actual act of cognition?

It is essential to realize that this bringing-forth must also be immediately given. Deduction must not be necessary in order to recognize it. This at once indicates that sense impressions do not meet our requirements, for we cannot know directly but only indirectly that sense impressions do not occur without activity on our part; this we discover only by considering physical and physiological factors. But we know quite immediately that concepts and ideas arise only through cognitive activity and through this enter the sphere of the directly given. In this respect concepts and ideas do not deceive anyone. A hallucination may appear as something externally given but we would never take our concepts to be something given without our thinking activity. (p. 94)

The conceptual framework by which we grasp an object of consciousness is our way of understanding that object – "the way it seems to me" – and we are never in the dark about this. We have direct intuition due to the fact that understanding entails our own activity: we feel ourselves actively *meaning* our understanding, and what we call "I" is always the identity actively meaning. This is why Steiner remarks, "this bringing-forth must also be immediately given." Thus while we may not know whether our understanding is correct, we always know what it is because we know what we *mean.*

But of course our list of possible contents of the given field included concepts and ideas, elements that fit the postulate. In fact, sorted by the distinction of what we do and what we suffer, the given will present two forms of content: a content given passively, which is not intelligible in itself, and a content which, while formally part of the given, is only *given* through our own intending activity. This latter element, in which our activity "finds itself active in the very essence of the given," Steiner names "concepts and ideas."

> It is a characteristic feature of the rest of the world-content that it must be *given* if we are to experience it; the only case in which the opposite occurs is that of concepts and ideas: *these we must bring forth if we are to experience them.* (p. 94)

The postulation that some part of the given must be immediately intelligible narrowed the examination to the part of the given produced by our own activity, namely, "concepts and ideas." These are produced by our own activity, but, once produced, meet us as part of the given – that is, they are directly presented in some sense to our mental gaze – even if their relation to the rest of the given (which is given passively) is not yet clear. The point is immediately followed by an argument that ideas are in fact *present* to the mind:

> Concepts and ideas alone are given to us in a form that is called *intellectual intuition (intellektuelle Anschauung)*. Kant and the later philosophers who follow in his steps completely deny this ability to humans, because it is said that all thinking refers only to objects and does not itself produce anything. In intellectual intuition the content must be contained within the thought-form itself. But is this not precisely the case with pure concepts and ideas? (p. 94)

"By concept," begins the following parenthetical qualification that now interrupts the passage, "I mean a principle according to which the unconnected elements of perception are bound into a unity." If we compare this to the earlier footnote, which reads: "Differentiation of the undifferentiated given into individual entities is already a result of cognitive activity," Steiner's remarks make the concept both something that may be experienced in itself, and the means by which we take notice of anything else. The latter point is illustrated with a brief reinterpretation of the Humean problem of causality, which was the occasion of an earlier disagreement with Kant.

> One need only look at them [concepts and ideas] in the form which they possess while they are still free of all empirical content. If one wants to grasp the pure concept of causality, then one must not hold to a particular instance, nor even to the sum of instances, but only the concept itself. Causes and effects we must seek in the world, but we must produce *causality* as a thought-form before we can look for the relation in the world. If one wanted to cling to the Kantian dictum that concepts without perceptions are empty, one could not think of determining the "given" world through concepts. Let us imagine that two elements of the world, *a* and *b* are "given." If I am to seek a relation between them I must do so with the help of a principle of definite content. I can only produce this through the act of cognition – I cannot take it from the objects as "given," for their relation is to be determined with the aid of this same principle. Such a principle, by which we determine reality, belongs only to a purely conceptual sphere. (p. 95)

It has been obvious, since the work of David Hume, that apparent causal relations are the result of our way of seeing. But that does not prevent us from "seeing" them – from having the sense that we plainly *saw* the thrown rock break the glass. But of course the rock's relation to the glass in not itself sensible, but conceptual. As Steiner remarks in his later *Philosophy of Freedom*, however, the concept is present *before* we grasp the phenomenal result. Thus when we hear a noise in the forest we must conceive the noise to be an *effect* before we can find it incomplete without a *cause,* and only this conceptualization allows us to go in search of the latter (the cause). The activity of *looking for* portrayed here is the first stage of a description that will expand into the following chapter.

At the end of step two we have fastened on the concepts and ideas produced by our own activity as the starting point. But this necessitates that we advance conceptual intentions before the event of recognition, while the usual understanding of everyday thought is to suppose that the concept is somehow derived from the recognition. The results of the investigation, however, are as yet too condensed. We must now ask how these conceptual intentions relate to the other type of content in the given field –• that is, the *other than thinking* that is passively given. It will be left to chapter five to show that from such a starting point the remaining activity of cognition can be successfully described.

Cognition and Reality

The first paragraphs of the new chapter appear even more condensed than the first paragraphs of the preceding arguments. "Concepts and ideas," Steiner begins, comprise part of the given, but at the same time lead beyond it. This makes it possible to determine the nature of the remaining activity of cognition. (p. 96)

They "lead beyond" because our activity of thinking can take hold at just this point. But the required neutral description has left us with a field populated by two species of given: the "other than thinking," which we cannot comprehend, and the products of thinking, which we can. A determination of the "remaining activity of cognition" will consist in establishing the proper relations within the given field, explaining how the other than thinking is to be grasped.

It may seem strange to refer to "concepts and ideas" in a given but unrelated condition, when we usually think of them think of them in an applied situation – that is, a concept is a concept *of* something, and thus at least related to that thing. But since "things" are not recognized until they are conceptualized, the concept is treated in another manner here: "By concept I mean a principle by which the unconnected elements of perception are bound into a unity." Obviously the phrase "unconnected elements" does not refer to individual pieces, for each of these would already possess a unity, but it refers to that content of the given field that shall become unified as the concept is applied. Thus, the concept must be produced before it can be applied. (This argument is expanded in the "Interruption" on intentionality below.)

Although Steiner has removed the distinction between objective and subjective from his starting point, the current prejudice that thinking must be merely subjective requires a specific argument to avoid this impression. Thus in the second paragraph Steiner warns that we must realize that the distinction just made between the two types of given content is "artificial" with respect to the given:

> Through a postulate we have separated a particular part from the rest of the given content; this was done because it lies in the nature of cognition to start with just this part. Thus it was separated only to allow us to understand the act of cognition. In so doing we must be clear that we have artificially torn apart the unity of the world-content. We must realize that what we have separated has a necessary connection to that content irrespective of our postulate. (p. 96)

This is a new argument and one that can be particularly difficult for the unprepared reader to absorb. The point is that there must be a determinate relation between the *passively given* "other than thinking" and the *intentionally given,* which relation our investigation must discover. In order to do this Steiner must complete his description of intentional activity. The paragraph continues:

> This provides the next step in the theory of knowledge; it must consist of restoring that unity which we tore apart in order to make knowledge possible. This restoration takes place in thinking of the world as given. Our thinking contemplation of the world brings about the actual union of the two parts of the world content: the part we survey as

given on the horizon of our experience, and the
part that has to be produced in the act of cognition
before it also can be given. The act of cognition is
the synthesis of these two elements. Indeed, in
every single act of cognition, one part appears as
something produced in this act itself, and it is
brought by the same act to the merely given. (p. 96)

Thus the *"idea of cognition"* makes its first appearance, and we
enter step three. The activity of cognition now appears to be the
mediation of one content by another – that is, when presented with a
passively given content, cognition cannot proceed unless it produces a
contribution of its own in order to mediate (or recognize) the former.
Knowledge – or consciousness, which always implies some form of
knowledge – must arise from this mediation, Steiner concludes, if it is to
arise at all. But as the previous chapter established, the demand for this
mediation comes from the particular nature of thinking:

To permeate the "given" world with concepts and
ideas is a *thinking* contemplation of things. Thus
thinking is actually the act through which
knowledge is mediated. Only when thinking, out of
itself, orders the content of the world picture, can
knowledge come about. Thinking itself is an
activity that brings forth a content of its own in
the moment of knowing. Insofar as the content
that is cognized issues from thinking, it contains
no problems for cognition. We have only to
observe it: the very nature of what we observe is

given to us directly. A description of thinking is also at the same time the science of thinking. Logic too has always been a description of thought forms, never a science that demonstrates anything. Demonstrative evidence is only called for when the content of thought is synthesized with some other content of the world ... with thinking, all demonstration [that is, providing evidence] ceases, for demonstration presupposes thinking. One may be able to demonstrate a particular fact, but no one is able to demonstrate the validity of demonstration. We can only describe what demonstration is. In logic all theory is empiricism – in this science there is only observation. (p. 96)

In the preceding chapter Steiner had remarked that we are given the concept (by our own act) in such a manner that "the content is contained within the thought form itself." This is why he had to insist that the content given (intended) by thinking was the content with which thinking could make a start, where, that is, thinking "finds itself active in the very essence of the given." The term "observation" in the passage above appears to refer to this grasp of thought by thinking, the former being transparent to the latter.

But this "start" was a beginning of a knowledge of the other-than-thinking, and so now Steiner must extend his description to that part, completing the idea of cognition:

But when we want to know something other than thinking, we can do so only with the help of thinking

– that is, thinking has to approach something given and transform its chaotic relationship with the world picture into a systematic one. Thinking therefore approaches the given content as an organizing principle. The process takes place as follows: Thinking first lifts out certain entities from the totality of the world-whole. In the given there is actually no singularity, for all is continuously blended. Then thinking relates these separate entities to each other in accordance with the thought-forms it produces, and lastly determines the outcome of this relationship. When thinking restores a relationship between two separate sections of the world-content, it does not do so arbitrarily. Thinking waits for what comes to light of its own accord as a result of restoring the relationship. It is this result alone which is knowledge of that particular section of the world content. If the latter were unable to express anything about itself through that relationship, then this attempt made by thinking would fail, and one would have to try again. All knowledge depends on establishing a correct relationship between two or more elements of reality, and comprehending the result of this. (p. 97)

Most readers will have noticed the unusual nature of this account. This is the direct investigation of mental activity that Kant failed to make, and it has, as Steiner's first chapter intimated, radically changed the problem of knowledge.

First Interruption: The Concept of Intentionality

46

At this point there are so many potential difficulties with Steiner's mode of expression that certain aspects of the argument probably need historical expansion. Steiner is working within a tradition of German thought which allows him to assume some familiarity with the work of Kant and his successors, in particular, that of Fichte, which he will review in chapter six. It was Fichte who called attention to the element of will in "the action of intelligence." He pointed out that in order to perceive a relation the mind had to entertain willfully that same relation – to "set it forth" *(setzen)* or, as it is usually translated, to "posit" it. Steiner speaks of the "bringing-forth" or "productive" *(hervorbringen)* activity of thinking in chapters four and five, but in chapter six he passes over into Fichte's language, and instead of *hervorbringen* he will utilize *setzen*, translating his argument into Fichte's terminology.

Such "positing" is not a statement in words, but an activity that precedes and prepares for all recognitions, and which may only be detected by inward inspection of perception. The long introspective descriptions of our willful activity within ordinary perceptual life of Johannes Muller's *Handbuch der Physiologie des Menschen* (1830) follow on his studies of Fichte's work, although von Muller changed the term "posit" to "intend" in order to avoid confusing the activity with verbal claims. (In an independent development Edmund Husserl would also use "intention" to name this activity. I will also adopt it, for in the present intellectual climate Steiner's "thinking" will be mistaken for "thinking in propositions.")

The description in the *Handbuch* is still one of the most accessible introductions to the subject. Reminding his reader of the nature of everyday experience, Muller points out that

> if the attention is withdrawn from the senses but
> immersed in intellectual exercise, in speculation or deep

passion, the soul completely disregards sensations. They are not noticed at all, they do not reach the consciousness of the ego ...

If this is so, then it follows that in order for sensation to reach consciousness, the attention that Muller has just described as "withdrawn" must be restored. Substituting "intention" for "attention" from time to time, Muller continues with examples of the manner in which we organize the reports of our senses according to how we approach them with our intentional activity:

When we are looking at a geometric figure we can successively focus on individual elements and ignore the rest without changing the visual axis ... The effect of intention is different with our hearing, which does not differentiate between spatial extensions like vision and tactile senses, but has the strongest perception of the sequence of impressions. It is amazing how we can pick out the weakest sounds. Usually we ignore the weak second accents of the strings and other instruments. With attention, we accentuate their perception ... Stranger yet is the capacity to hear each sound out of simultaneously-heard sounds of an orchestra by intention and to be able to follow the weakest sounds of an instrument attentively while the impression of others diminishes.

Another recognizable experience is the "double-take" alluded to above, in which the observer, through the failure of ordinary perception, becomes aware of his or her activity in making a correction. Of course, normal seeing is so successful that our activity is totally transparent to what we are looking at and we do not notice it. But when our attempt to see fails, we are forced to look a second time to make sense of the situation. Now, after the fact, we become aware that we have been active in producing an experience: the first "take" becomes our "mis-take," and if we were somehow responsible for it, we must also be responsible for the second, and correct, "take." Such examples are part of everyday experience, but in themselves they only show that mental activity must contribute something if perception is to arise. Due to the short duration of the first "take," however, it is difficult to examine how a "mediation" by the observer can unify the passively given. Thus we need better examples.

Figure 1

Let us examine, for our example, the effort needed to see the image or images hidden in the very grainy photograph in Figure 1, if one has never seen it before.

As we examine the photograph, we may see a rock (or a tortoise) in the lower right foreground, perhaps a bird or small animal sitting on it, some sort of dark object in the upper left which seems to extend toward us as it extends toward the middle of the field, some tree branches in the upper right – etc. But these images are seen only "suggestively," like the cloud that Hamlet asks Polonius to see as a camel, a weasel, and a whale, successively. They are not really recognizable objects, but only proposals that cannot be completely realized. This is, in fact, the result I was expecting, for I have not placed the photograph right side up. I would suggest that the reader try rotating the piece, looking for a good image. Oddly enough, although at first everything looks like mere possibility and suggestion, once the image is found the viewer will have no doubts. We can recognize a good image even in a bad photograph.

Once the reader is ready to receive directives, I can add that the plate should be turned so that the Figure 1 caption is on the left side reading downward, and the picture is a photograph of a common animal.

If these directives do not produce an image (I remember that they did not work for me when I met the photograph for the first time), let me add that the animal is a cow, looking right at the reader, the head almost filling the left half of the plate. This final and most effective directive consists mainly of the name, but the name often produces quick results because one is already familiar with the animal looking for the familiar form enables one to look for the named object, which activity evidently prepares for actual recognition.

The activity of the perceiver is similar to that mentioned in the experience of the orchestra above, in which one could focus upon one type of instrument and allow the others to become background. When we look for the sound of the flutes, they stand out for us. But this step of recognition now appears somewhat mysterious since prior to recognition of a possible object (of consciousness), we cannot consciously move our attention to it. After all, *the* cow is *not even a locatable unity* – a dark or light blur for instance – until we see it. But when seen it appears as a whole – we can even "see" the edge of the cow's face where there is no variation of brightness to allow us to do so. We do not see an object and recognize it as a cow, we look for a cow and therefore see a recognizable object. The unity has been provided by the concept proposed for our search. This is why Steiner calls the concept the element that provides a unity *to appearances.*

Thus it now seems that conceptual action is required of us *before* we can fasten on an image. We cannot, after all, move our attention to the head of the cow while it is not even an object – that is, has no unity even as a blur. Without our recognition as a cow, it is impossible to pick out the object. Between the time when the cow is not visible and the time when it is, our mental act has to provide the unity that makes it visible.

This requirement can be investigated in diagrams with far fewer elements. Take, for instance, the figure designed by Gaetano Kanisza, (1976) which produces a perception of a central white triangle by simply arranging the black circles with sections missing and three bent lines on a white background. The observer sees, apparently immediately, a white triangle in the center of the configuration, due to the manner in which the forms have been understood. Here is a case where the understanding that produces a consciousness of the white triangle can be reconstructed.

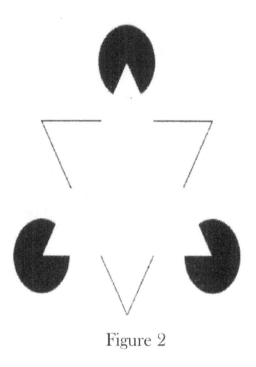

Figure 2

As the reader can verify, if the white triangle is seen, the underlying forms are grasped as closed, that is, the three black circles are complete and the bent lines are part of a continuous triangle. The foreground triangle lies over these forms and thus interrupts them. This triangle will appear somewhat brighter than the rest of the background, but the reader can mask off all but two elements – a circle and a bent line – and see these elements as nothing more than a black circle with a piece missing and a bent line. When they appear as nothing more, there is no hint of a brighter triangle. Thus the conceptual *closure* of the black form is a necessary condition for the appearance of the white one.

Another Kanisza effect is the transparent surface. In Figure 3 below, the white rectangle in front of the black forms is produced in the same manner as the white triangle of Figure 2. But if the dark forms are closed with a gray rather than black continuation, the white rectangle becomes transparent or translucent, as in Figure 4. In this case, as in the former, the rectangle can appear to be brighter than the surround, but here the rectangle has the quality of a very different substance – such as translucent white plastic or tissue paper.

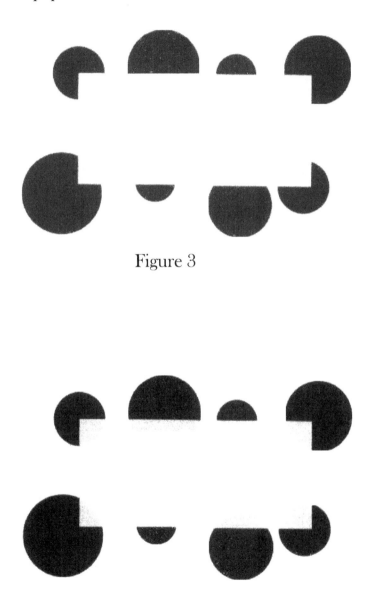

Figure 3

Figure 4

The translucent figure, of course, arises in much the same manner as the original white rectangle – that is, seeing a rectangle provides a parsimonious understanding of the gray areas – an understanding must be *seen* if it is to apply.

The temptation to suppose that we see the rectangle first and understand it later – that is, to suppose it appears without any participation from thinking, and our mental activity takes hold after the fact, can be dissipated with a simple experiment. Let the viewer attempt to grasp the black areas as holes – in something like a slice of Swiss cheese – and see, through the holes, a gray rectangle. Once the gray rectangle is seen as a background figure, the apparent brightness of the foreground rectangle has vanished. The new conceptualization of Figure 4 produces a new figure, which, of course, can be converted back into the old figure by a return to the old understanding.

For a further examination the reader may simply relax and stare at any of these configurations without concern for a geometric understanding. In this "vegetating" mood, the design elements seem to "swim" slightly and appear as nothing more than separate elements on paper – for instance, three bent lines and three black circles with slices missing, or eight circles divided into gray and black areas. But the slightest attempt to make sense of the whole – that is, to put everything into understandable spatial relation – will return the viewer to the missing figure.

Let me review the ground carefully. As argued above, the viewer must grasp the black elements as closed in order to obtain the figure-ground separation that allows the white triangle to be the foreground. But obviously this conception must be in place by the time we become consciousness of the white triangle or white rectangle. It is a condition

54

by which we become conscious of the form, and not something added to the resulting phenomenon. Yet in the viewer's experience the white form is usually "there" from the beginning. The understanding is usually advanced before we are conscious of advancing it, since, until a unified target is perceived, we would not be aware of any necessity to advance it. (Only in the case of our deliberate reconstruction of Figure 4 are we aware of making a proposal before we see the result.)

Counter-intuitively, the act of recognition lies in our activity immediately *anterior* to the fact of recognition. (By "anterior" I always mean "causally prior," and sometimes chronologically as well.) The objects mentioned are already closed at first notice. The understanding of them as closed, therefore, must already be in place when our first experience of them is obtained. The same is true, of course, of the closure of the three-dimensional objects of our usual surroundings. They appear closed in immediate perception, even though their shape is often interrupted by that of other objects and, most strikingly, they extend invisibly *away* from the viewer to achieve the three-dimensional volume that we immediately feel in their concrete presence. Our intention has obviously preceded that experience.

It is easy to mistake this point. We are so determined to believe that we see the world first and understand it second that most observers – including scientific observers – simply do not notice that *there cannot be a distinction* between perceiving a relation and understanding the relation. This prejudice is very widespread and very strong. We all know, for example, that we can generate a mistaken perception of the world through our experience of double-takes, and that any examination of such a perceptual shift will reveal an underlying shift in relations, yet the notion that a double-take is cognitively driven (intentionally produced) rather than an "error of sense" will often be missed. One must make a concerted effort to notice his or her activity of "taking notice" if intentional activity is to be raised to consciousness.

The usual assumption that "attending to" something is only a matter of the focus of the eyes is obviously an error, absurdly transparent when we try the same reasoning on the ears. Taking Müller's example, although we can focus on different sounds in the general background of sound, can anyone suggest that this ability to pick out the flutes from the orchestra rests on the physical orientation of the ears? A cursory examination of how we pass from one sound to another easily reveals the point: we attend by specifying – conceiving – the type of sound we want to hear. As soon as we succeed, the individual sound leaps out. Or fails to leap out, for we can also verify the absence of a particular instrument through the same intentional specification. When someone remarks, while listening to recorded music, that the timpani seem to be absent, we verify the claim by *listening for* the timpani. Had we not listened specifically, we could not have heard that it was absent. By implication, if we did not know how to listen specifically to an instrument, we might never detect its presence within the combined orchestral sound.

Memory

Of course, it must seem to some readers that they specify an instrument, or a shape, by calling up a *memory* of the same. Thus it seems that I remember what trumpets sound like and then listen for that sound, or I remember what a certain shape looks like and then look for that shape. But the thesis that recognition is just remembering is possible to accept only by forgetting everything we have already examined. The view of remembering put forward in the memory account is based on a naive view of perception – the familiar notion that we see the world without cognitive activity and think about it later. Thus we suppose that memory re-presents the seen object unencumbered by conceptual activity. But as the argument above demonstrates, this is not possible.

Since we cannot see without recognition, we do not remember what has been seen (or heard) without the same activity. Simple observation of memory experience shows the difference between the original and the memory. Consider Figure 5.

If we ask an average audience, "what do you see?", some will reply that they see a cube slanting down and to the right, others a cube slanting up and to the left, others will say both. Eventually, of course, everyone will see both cubes. They will also be able to see a flat pattern, a truncated crystal from above (convex), or the same shape from below (concave), etc. They are able to do this by proposing differing depth relations to the elements in the diagram.

Of course, these differing configurations are not added by thought after the object is perceived, but are intended by the perceiver in the act of perception – that is, we must take the elements of the perceptual field to be at specific depths in order to see this or that figure. Even the flat pattern follows this rule,

for we cannot reach it without seeing all elements on the same plane. But now close your eyes and refer to memory.

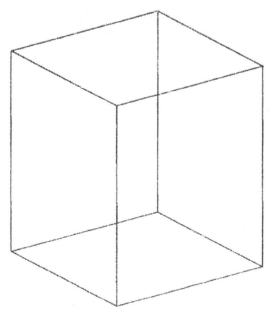

Figure 5

At once the experience of a given situation which can be seen in more than one way disappears. What we remember are the various ways that we saw it – the results of previous conceptual unifications. The condition of an original given – that is, allowing multiple appearances – cannot be re-experienced through memory. Memory is not equivalent to a confrontation with the "other than thinking. " As Hume noted, it lacks the "vividness" of direct sensation, and this same "vividness" enables the intentional act to produce a result. But only this result can be remembered.

Our awareness of this limitation is derived from the fact that we understand – even as we know that intentional activity is produced by us – that in sensible perception we are meeting something that is not so produced, and we cannot objectify our intentions without it. Our intentional activity cannot create such a reality – no amount of mere intending will produce the sensible content of perception. Thus we suffer the limitations that sensible content enforces on our ways of viewing. After all, if we do not produce a way of looking that "fits" (in some sense) this *other-than-thinking,* no intelligible picture will result. This limitation is not derived from thinking, but imposed upon thinking by the directly given.

It is this element, of course, which provides our sense *that* something is there to look at, although the *what* is entirely derived from the intentional proposal through which we look. The *other-than-thinking* does not guide our intention by providing relations on its own, but by failing to appear unless we view it – or intend it – through adequate intentions. Thus if we were to ask "what does this figure look like prior to all intentional contribution?" it should now be clear that it has no *look* at all. And having no look, it also possesses no "outness" – it is not an object "out there," for no relations like "in" and "out" are yet established. Its otherness is completely exhausted by its independence of intentional activity – by the fact that we must suffer rather than produce it. We can bring the given to appearance only through our own intentional activity, but without the element that is only suffered there is nothing to appear.

By reflection on the above observations one may hypothesize that in order to "perceive" anything the perceiver must (1) mediate the sensible situation with an intentional contribution, and (2) observe the result, which now becomes a new given. There are two important conclusions here.

The first is the rejection of the supposed simplicity of the perceptual moment. This impression derives from the fact that our intentional activity is a necessary preparation not only for perception but also, by implication, for consciousness itself. We can become aware only of intelligible objects (in the grammatical sense), which objects can only be the result of intentional mediation. Since our productive activity is prior to consciousness – *which will be the result* – when this result is unproblematic we have no sense of a preparatory moment. From the unconscious character of our own activity we derive the impression of simplicity. Yet when a proposed mediation fails (the double-take), it becomes obvious after the fact that our own tacit activity was at work, and we recognize that we are called upon to make a change in that activity.

The second conclusion, which follows from the preceding one, is that proposing an intention is not the same as seeing a satisfactory result. We do not create the world, but only its intelligible appearance, which is our knowledge of it. Thus we discover that an unsatisfactory proposal will not result in fully intelligible phenomena, and we are obliged to try again. Obviously the success of our activity is not measured subjectively, but by how intelligibly it can reveal a given.

The "two moment" hypothesis begins to show its truth as soon as we begin to look at our perceptive act in these terms. As we investigate Figure 1 and perceive the suggestive figures, the bird, the rock, etc., we do so by looking for them – that is, by conceiving this or that blot as a bird or a rock.

When, as in Figure 5, we see distinct alternative images, we dismiss the possibility that the printed figure is changing, as we dismiss this same possibility in the double-take and locate the change in the observer. With practice we can confirm that, as different images succeed each other, we have been active in preparing each change, for each new image now appears as our "taking" rather than something independent of us. Yet we do not suppose, for that reason, that we are creating our perceptions. After all, *a proposal may fail.* One may look for (intend) rounded forms, for example, or triangular ones, but nothing comes of this. It is therefore obvious that our activity produces only intentional proposals, which are clearly distinguished from perceptual results – that is, actual perceptions. (Memory, of course, can now be seen to be limited to the re-presentation of actual perceptions.)

Now if the activity of intentionality must precede any phenomenal result, then it also follows that *all phenomena are cognitions* – are a unity of intention and sensation. The spatial relations in which we contextualize the sensible situation of Figure 4 are the very geometrical concepts by which we grasp the resulting configuration. Phenomena can appear only to a mode of understanding by which we think, or mean, them, and we must mean them before they become apparent. Phenomenal appearance emerges as a kind "mirroring" of the intended relations, which must reflect back to the thinker his or her own intention, but now individualized and concrete. *At the moment of actuality the phenomenon and the understand-ing by which it is recognized are not separable.*

I have spent a good deal of time on intentionality due to my impression that Steiner's epistemological arguments cannot be understood without a sense of *thinking* that is intentional rather than propositional. In doing so, however, I have run slightly ahead of the textual argument. The relations I have covered above will take on greater significance in Steiner's treatment.

Return: Chapter Five

Now let us return to the beginning of chapter five, and the warning that we have "torn apart" the world content. The argument is condensed in Steiner's terse comments. Reflection will show that as we examine our own cognition we become aware of two components. To perceive we must receive the object of perception according to our own nature, that is, through two distinct modes of acquisition, and thus the "tearing apart" of the content into two contents. Thus we can only approach the object of perception by joining the contents of these two receptions, mediating the passive given with the intentionally given.

But (and here is the point), though this distinction between what is given to us passively and what is given intentionally is important for our understanding of our act of cognition, it may be termed "artificial" with regard to the resulting content of perception. By the time we observe the outcome of successful intentional activity, the two given contents have become one, revealing the "necessary relation" they bear to each other according to their own nature. After all, in normal experience we become aware of a difference between them only when our proposal does not illumine the given – that is, our proposed organization fails.

The fact that the two parts of the given are only distinct "parts" when we speak of a failed cognitive act, or when we distinguish content according to the mode of reception, should give us pause with regard to the usual assumptions concerning cognition. After all, *thinking* (intentional activity) has not as yet been revealed by this investigation as either subjective or transsubjective, although we are now in a position to address that question.

Faced with the necessity of combining two contents in order to come by a phenomenal appearance, the investigator can take this structure in one of two ways: either the separation of the two forms of given is original and their unity a derived condition arising through our activity, or the union of the two is original, and their separation a derived condition produced by our modes of reception. The usual epistemological assumption would prescribe the former answer; we suppose that we have added our mental contribution to something which is already complete without it. This conclusion then necessitates some further justification for the addition of the intentional element.

But if we attempt to solve this question by evidence rather than assumption, only a direct observation of the given contents themselves can reveal their relation. This is possible only when both are given – that is, is, when we have a phenomenal result. In the phenomena, the relation between the intentionally given and the passively given – a relation that belongs to the phenomena rather than to the conditions of cognition – is *unity.* The phenomena are indifferent to the manner in which they have been obtained and give no sign of being partitioned according to our modes of reception.

This is one of the junctions at which Steiner's transition from a *transcendental* to an *immanent* formulation of the problem of epistemology pays rich dividends. Obviously, if we were asking how our thinking applied to the reality independent of our senses, we would have no way of arguing that it applied at all. But now the whole problem of cognition is set by our passive reception of something other than thinking, which does not possess organizing relations and therefore is not intelligible in itself. We can only be asking, therefore, about whether our proposal has produced intelligible appearances.

We all know about the situations in which we find our grasp less than satisfactory. Ambiguous pictures lack stability and can be seen in several different ways equally well. Certain problematic art works, including the interesting designs of Escher, refuse intelligibility in that we cannot complete them – something is always wrong. And the original take of the double-take also had something wrong with it or we would never have moved to a second take. What we cannot unify remains unintelligible to just the degree that it is not unified. Upon reflection, however, this unity to which I refer must be the unity between the intentional given and the passive given.

When we turn away from these questionable circumstances and consider the "normal" case of intelligible perception, our experience is quite different. Here the impression of unity is so strong we are not usually aware of any hint of observer contribution in immediate appearances. For the observer who considers no other cases than those of immediate intelligibility, the partition between what we produce and what is given passively appears to fall between the perception and what follows – that is, between the phenomenon and our thought about it. Thus we find, in a 1964 text by H. H. Price entitled *Perception:* "The perceptual act ... is not an activity. There is in it no element of fussiness, no wondering nor questioning. One does not have to take trouble over it – it is a blessed relief from the labor of discursive thought." Although Price is the author of a text on the subject, his own position with regard to perception is naïve. His remarks are directed entirely toward the result of successful perception, and he has missed the moment that prepares for perception. By failing to distinguish the proposal from result, he has ignored the possibility of failure, and as we shall see below, the omission precludes an account of success. The naïve approach makes epistemology impossible by occluding the moment that a form of judgment is applied to our perceptual activity.

Those who penetrate these moments – as we have done with the exercise above, or as anyone does when examining their own experience of the double-take – become aware of an activity that works within them. By contrast, the Price text describes the phenomenal result as if it had no ancestry. He emphasizes only the nature of this outcome – the fact *that the unity of the phenomenon is seamless.*

Not so the cognitive act, to which we must now return. We can easily see that in the act of perception our own activity meets something other than itself. In fact, we understand that if it did not, there would be no reality to encounter. But the popular notion that our concepts must add something to reality arises from the assumption that the concept is applied to actual phenomena – entitles complete and specific in themselves. Yet when we pass from phenomena to the precognitive given, we come to a content that does require a conceptual addition, for it never appears as something complete in itself and cannot become specified in itself. In fact we become aware of it only through our

64

inability to objectify our concepts – to gain evidence that something is present – without it.

If the element "already present" cannot self-specify, it may be said to be alienated from its own unity; how else could the unity that belongs to it be given through our activity? Such a condition can be brought about only through our mode of receptivity, and thus it could occur only in the act of cognition. The distinction between two types of given which is found in the first stage of cognition, therefore, has no bearing on the resulting knowledge, which is identical with the phenomena.

If we now reread Steiner's description of the act of cognition we may be able to find more in it than we could on first reading. For one thing, there is a strong emphasis upon the notion of observation in this account, and an expansion of its usual meaning. Steiner begins the long descriptive paragraph with a generalization:

> To permeate the "given" world with concepts and ideas is a *thinking* contemplation of things. Thus thinking is the act through which knowledge is mediated. Only when thinking, out of itself, orders the content of the world picture, can knowledge come about. (p. 96)

Since we can now see that without intentional mediation – the work of thinking – the world would not come to phenomenal appearance, the point of his claim is well taken. If thinking does not order the world, it cannot come to consciousness at all. But before explaining the process by which thinking can be brought to "permeate" the given, Steiner gives an account of observing, not the world, but thinking.

Thinking itself is an activity that brings forth a content

of its own in the moment of cognition. Insofar as the content that is cognized issues from thinking, it contains no problems for cognition. We have only to observe it: the essence is given to us directly. A description of thinking is also at the same time the science of thinking. Logic too has always been a description of thought forms, never a science that demonstrates anything ... In logic all theory is empiricism – in this science there is only observation. (p. 96)

The sense of "observation" here is of course quite distinct from that of ordinary empiricism. Here the "essence of what we observe is given to us directly" because "thinking finds itself active in the very essence of the given." As I suggested, "observation" here denotes the grasp of thought by thinking, the former being transparent to the latter. But we should realize that the argument occupies this position in the paragraph because it is a necessary background for the description that follows. The next sentence turns toward the problem of cognizing that which is other than thinking, basically repeating the point that introduced the paragraph:

> But when we want to know something other than thinking, we can do so only with the help of thinking – that is, thinking has to approach something given and transform the chaotic relationship with the world picture into a systematic one. Thinking therefore approaches the given content as an organizing principle. (p. 96)

But now Steiner adds a description of how this is done:

> The process takes place as follows: Thinking first lifts out
> certain entities from the totality of the world-whole. In the
> given there is actually no singularity for all is continuously
> blended. Then thinking relates these separate entities to each
> other in accordance with the thought-forms it produces, and
> lastly determines what results from this relation. (p.

Notice that having "lifted out" singular entities, presumably by
conceptualizing their unity ("By concept I mean the principle by which
the disconnected elements of perception are bound into a unity"), we
have created another form of a lack of unity – that is, multiplicity. But
again the conceptual principle is advanced in order to bind into
relation – like that of cause and effect – or unify (by placing in
relation). But we cannot legislate the relation we propose, but must
rather wait upon a result: "thinking ... lastly determines what results
from this relation." Our attention is here directed to the separate
moment in which the result of our proposal of relation is examined,
and this moment is crucial to the cognitive act. It is on this basis that
Steiner denies the Kantian formulation.

> By establishing a relation between two distinct parts of the
> world content, thinking of itself has determined absolutely
> nothing about them. Thinking waits for what comes to light *of
> its own accord* as a result of restoring the relationship. *It is this
> result alone* that is knowledge of that particular section of the
> world content. (p. 97, emphasis mine)

The possibility of an arbitrary assignment of relation is a reference to skepticism in general and Kant in particular, who had supposed that because concepts were given by our own activity they were also determined purely by our own subjectivity (actually a worry central to Western thought since the nominalism of William of Ockham.) Yet since the object of our knowledge is something other than thinking, it would seem obvious that we could not decide which concepts would properly apply until we knew the role played by the passively given content in this determination. Kant could never assign any clear role to the "sensible manifold" as he termed it, but Steiner's account adds to that very element.

The process of cognition is not arbitrary because it is not the proposal of relation that decides whether a relation is correct or no, but the observation of "what comes to light of its own accord as a result of restoring the relationship." Remember that the passive given has been produced by stripping away the relations that belong to it, and our attempt to understand is an attempt to *restore* those same relations. The productive aspect of thinking is the proposal of relations; this moment *can* be subjective, and if we saw nothing else we would harbor suspicions that our concepts were arbitrary. Only in the subsequent moment that I termed "observation" is the suitability or unsuitability of the intentional proposal revealed, and "it is this result alone" – that is, "what comes to light of its own accord" – that is knowledge.

"Thinking waits for" something that is transparent to it, something that it can therefore *observe*. We have already been given the model of thinking "observing" thought, and a successful intentional mediation has a phenomenal result that is also like unto thought – has the form of thought and is immediately intelligible to us – with this difference, however, that it is what Kant called "the sensible manifold" that shows that something has been perceived, or that it has not. After all, what now "comes to light of its own accord" is not our intentional proposal, but what became evident as a result of that activity.

This is why Steiner now speaks of an enabling of the object of knowledge rather than our cognitive activity:

> If this particular section of the world content *were unable* to express anything about itself through that relationship, then this attempt made by thinking would fail, and one would have to try again. (p. 97, emphasis mine)

We have nothing more to do but observe. If we have chosen suitable relations, an object of observation will now express something about itself through the relations we propose. Our thinking activity was only a precondition for a self-expression that was not our own: it proposes, but another element disposes. No other element meets our proposals but the passive given, but we must remember that this element cannot be observed in its original form. What we now observe is not the original form of the given, but the transformation of the same brought about by our intentional mediation which, by this account, restores the relations originally stripped away by our mode of reception. If what now comes to light is intelligible, its intelligibility is similar to the intelligibility of thought to thinking. But it is now *the object of knowledge*, rather than either of the two types of given, which here becomes manifest, and decides the matter.

The basic description of cognition's dual movement – receiving the world in a fragmentary condition and then reunifying it – has been put forward in such general terms that it is easily extended to the entirety of science. The problem of acquiring an object of cognition was brought about by our reception of the object without its concept, which we must restore through our own activity. The problems of science –

69

the relations of phenomena – can be understood as an expression of the same difficulty. By perceiving "separate" entities we have actually reformulated the "artificial" condition on a new level. The separate things are discrete because we have called them into phenomenal appearance without the network of relations of which they are an expression. On every level of science it is the incomplete nature of our own perceptual process that we strive to overcome:

> All knowledge depends on establishing a correct relationship between two or more elements of reality and grasping the result of this. (p. 97)

"Grasping" (erfassen), that is, observing, for the "result" is a new given.

From this general statement of the activity of cognition Steiner brings his argument back to the original experience of intentionality as it is embedded in everyday recognition:

> There is no doubt that many of our attempts to grasp things by means of thinking fail; this is apparent not only in the history of science, but also in ordinary life; it is just that in the simple cases we usually encounter, the right concept replaces the wrong one so quickly that the latter does not come to consciousness at all or does so only seldom. (p. 97)

Of course the passage depends, for its persuasiveness, on our memory of the time that we did notice the replacement of one concept by another – that is, the "double-take." In the light of the entire discussion above, the "double-take" is a privileged moment. Within it an appearance almost becomes but falls short – fails in its unity. Because our activity is no longer transparent to its object, we become aware of that activity, aware that we have made a mis-take, and aware that the new and more successful appearance that follows was the result of a new "take" on our part. The whole episode suggests that our activity achieves its end only in our detection of intelligible appearances. The phenomenon is the goal of our search, which search can only be quenched in perceiving – that is, knowing – even if the achievement, in the long run, is only temporary, since it will give rise to new problems.

Because the problem of knowledge is the same whatever the level of comprehension we take for its inception, Steiner sometimes begins his argument – as he does in *Goethe's Theory of Knowledge: An Outline of the Epistemology of His Worldview* – from what seem to be perceived but unrelated entities, and traces the manner in which thinking advances from that start. In the dissertation, however, the double-take is the paradigm case, for the argument postulates that discreet entities must first be lifted out of the given by thinking in order for the problem of their discreteness to exist.

Since his own account is now visible, Steiner turns to the work of Kant for contrast. The next paragraph:

> When Kant speaks of "the synthetic unity of apperception it is evident that he had some inkling of what we have shown here to be the activity of thinking, the purpose of which is to organize the world-content systematically. But that he thought to derive *a priori* laws of pure science from the rules according to which this synthesis takes place shows how little this inkling brought to his consciousness the

essential task of thinking. He did not realize that this synthetic activity of thinking is only a *preparation* for discovering actual natural laws. Suppose, for example, that we detach a content, *a,* and another content, *b,* from the given. If we are to gain knowledge of the law connecting *a* and *b,* then thinking must first relate *a* and *b* so that through this relationship the connection between them presents itself as given. The actual content of a law of nature is derived from the given, and the task of thinking is merely to provide an occasion for the natural law to become evident by placing the elements of the given in that relationship. No objective laws follow from the synthetic activity of thinking alone. (p. 97)

Kant did not, of course, attempt to investigate intentionality directly; that step was left to Fichte. But he had enough awareness of the situation to know that the mind needed concepts in order to see. Being unable to distinguish the moment of proposal from the moment of observation, he supposed that our concepts legislate the phenomenal reality they discern. That there was another role for thinking did not occur to him:

> The activity of thinking is only a formal one in bringing about our scientific world-picture, and it follows that no cognition can have content which is *a priori* – which is established prior to observation (and therefore divorced from the given). Content must rather be derived wholly from observation. In this sense all our knowledge

is empirical. Nor is it possible to see how it could be otherwise. Kant's judgments *a priori* are not cognition, but only postulates. In the Kantian sense one can always say: If a thing is to be the object of any kind of experience, then it must conform to certain laws. Laws in this sense are prescriptions that the subject prescribes for the objects. Yet one would expect that if we are to attain knowledge of the given it must be derived, not from the subject, but from the object.

Thinking says nothing *a priori* about the given; it produces the thought-forms on the basis of which the conformity to law of the phenomena becomes apparent *a posteriori*. (p. 98)

In the last pages of the chapter Steiner summarizes the argument he has made:

The act of cognition is possible only because something is hidden in the given which does not appear in its immediate aspect, but reveals itself only through the order that thinking brings to the given. What lies within the given before it has been elaborated by thought is not its full totality.

This becomes clearer when we consider more closely the factors pertinent to the act of cognition. The first of these is the given. That it is given is not a feature of the given, but an expression denoting its relation to the second factor in cognition. Thus what this given may be is completely undecided by this designation. In the act of cognition thinking finds the second factor: the conceptual content of the given, to be necessarily united with the given. We must ask ourselves: (1) Where does the separation between given and concept lie? (2) Where are they united? Both these questions have been answered in the preceding investigation. The separation exists solely in the act of cognition, the union lies in the given. It follows from this that the conceptual content is only a part of the given, and that the act of cognition consists in uniting the parts of the world picture that are given to it separately. (p. 99)

The chapter concludes:

Knowledge rests on the fact that the world-content is originally given to us in an incomplete form; it possesses an essential aspect beyond what is immediately offered. This second aspect of the world-content, which is not originally given, is revealed through thinking. That which appears to us as something separate in thinking, is therefore not empty form, but comprises the sum of those determinations (categories) that are the form of the rest of the world content. The world-content can be called reality only in the form it attains when the two aspects described above have been united through knowledge. (p. 99)

The arguments *contra* Kant and the final summation are justified by the preceding discussion, which was framed, as we now see, by its opposition to neo-Kantian assumptions. The next chapter, however, invokes another framework.

Second Interruption: Cross-Reference to Other Works

Now that the "idea of cognition" of the dissertation has been worked through and can stand on its own, the cross-referencing that I avoided earlier no longer threatens to raise problems. In fact, some reference to other works may provide a useful expansion of concepts central to the argument.

In *The Philosophy of Freedom* Steiner argues that the activity of thinking – the entertainment of concepts – is not merely conventional or subjective, but receptive: our intentional activity is actually an acquiescence to the possible forms of activity – the mind is to ideas," Steiner remarks, "as the eye is to light." And in chapter five:

> Thinking offers ... content to the percept, from the human world of concepts and ideas. In contrast to the content of the percept, which is given to us from without, the content of thinking appears inwardly. The form in which this first makes its appearance we will call intuition. Intuition is for thinking what observation is for the percept. Intuition and observation are the sources of our knowledge. An observed object of the world remains unintelligible to us until we have within ourselves the corresponding intuition that adds the part

of reality lacking in the percept. To anyone who is incapable of finding intuitions corresponding to the things, the full reality remains inaccessible. Just as the color-blind person sees only the differences in brightness without any color qualities, so can the person without intuition observe only unconnected perceptual fragments.

To explain a thing, to make it intelligible, means nothing else than to place it in the context from which it has been torn by the peculiar character of our organization as already described. A thing cut off from the world-whole does not exist. All isolating has only subjective validity for our organization ...

The enigmatic character of an object consists in its separateness. But this separation is of our own making and can, within the world of concepts, be overcome again. (pp. 73-74)

The nature of this "separation" follows from the steps taken to eliminate it. We bring the given into conceptual elaboration. The concept, *qua* concept, is always relatively general in its content. Careful introspection will show the reader that the intentional activity advanced toward a specific object produces only a context of relations within which the particular may be known (perceived). The contribution that the concept lacks, and the passively given content supplies, is particularity – not the evidence of what has been perceived, but that it has been perceived. Thus we find, in Steiner's commentaries on Goethe's scientific works (*Goethean Science,* 1988):

In order to gain some clarity here, one must go back to

the reason for contrasting the perception *(Anschauung)*, as something particular, with the concept, as something general.

One must ask the question: Wherein do the characteristic features of the particular actually lie? Can these be defined conceptually? Can we say: *This* conceptual unity must break up into this or that particular perceptible manifold? "No" is the very definite answer. The concept in itself does not grasp particularity at all. The latter must lie in elements that are altogether inaccessible to the concept as such. But since we do not know any intervening member between perception and concept – unless one wishes to introduce something like Kant's fantastic-mystical schemata, which could not be taken seriously today - these elements must belong to perception itself. The basis for particularizing cannot be derived from the concept but must be sought within perception itself. What constitutes the particularity of an object cannot be *grasped conceptually,* but only *perceived.* (p. 114)

In *The Philosophy of Freedom,* the term "percept" *(Wahrnehmung)* is used for "the object of observation" presented to cognition prior to conceptual elaboration. When the discussion of chapter five arrives at the direct question "what is the percept?", Steiner answers as if the question were identical to "what is particularity?"

What then is the percept? The question, asked in this general way, is absurd. A percept emerges always as something perfectly definite, as a concrete content. This content is directly given and is completely contained within the given. The only question one can ask concerning the given content is what is it beyond the percept – that is, what is it for thinking. The question concerning the "what" of a percept can, therefore, only refer to the conceptual intuition that corresponds to this percept. (p. 76)

Particularity and generality are not phenomena, but aspects of the same. "To exist," as a reality, is to possess both. Obviously the particularity of an object cannot be separated from the whatness of the object, so the privation of concept from percept happens only in cognition. The percept, in its first condition, is a product of the receptive faculty of the subject. In chapter six of *The Philosophy of Freedom*, Steiner remarks:

Percepts are determined through the subject. But at the same time the subject has in thinking the means for canceling this self-produced determination. (p. 102)

Although Steiner will occasionally call this operation a "synthesis" of concept and percept, his shorthand should not lead one to suppose that two entities are here being combined. The cancellation of separation cannot be a combination of two unities when that separation represents a distortion – a loss of unity. Let us say rather that the emancipation from the conditions of reception represents a transformation of the percept from its first form to that which, through conceptual elaboration, begins to reveal its true nature. It is really our own condition of ignorance that is being eliminated.

Upon reflection it would appear that our ingrained sense of the partitions of experience always refers back to our experience of the cognitive process – as we have seen in the case of the double-take – rather than the reality cognized. In our effort to cognize we become aware of the distinction between percept and concept, between particularity and generality. It may readily appear that all we can know through such elements must also consist of the same dichotomies. To make this inference, however, is to forget that the individual reality we discover in perception consists of a unity between percept and concept, between particularity and generality. As we actually know in the moment of perception, and must remember during later reflection, this is a unity that defies analysis. (Although we cannot here work out the extent to which this account is related to the Aristotelian distinctions between "form" and "matter", or "actual" and "potential," Steiner's other writings show that he was quite aware of such a relation.)

Finally, in order to avoid interruption of the next chapter, it will be instructive to look at Steiner's remarks about the "observation of thinking," at this point. The argument found in the *Philosophy* can be seen to follow from the description of cognition just reviewed, but the central insight makes its appearance in chapter 6 in a very different manner.

In chapter three of *The Philosophy of Freedom* Steiner remarks that "thinking as an object of observation differs essentially from all other objects" and continues to argue that an observation of thinking would be "an exceptional state," since thinking is normally the activity by which we contemplate everything other than our act of contemplation.

> The first observation that we make about thinking is therefore this: that it is the unobserved element in our ordinary mental life and spiritual life.
>
> The reason why we do not observe the thinking that goes on in our ordinary life is none other than this, that it is due to our own activity. Whatever I do not myself produce appears in my field of observation as an object; I find myself confronted by it as something that has come about independently of me. It comes to meet me. I must accept it as something that precedes my thinking process, as a premise. When I am thinking about the object I am occupied with it and my attention is focused upon it. To be this occupied is precisely to *contemplate by thinking.* I attend, not to my own activity, but to the object of this activity. I pay no heed to my thinking, which is of my own making, but only to the *object* of my thinking, which is not of my making. *(The Philosophy of Freedom*, pp. 26-27)

So far the argument seems concerned with habits of attention, and although such habits are involved here, the difficulty involved in the observation of thinking is more than simply breaking with our habits.

The next paragraphs read:

> I am, moreover, in the same position when I enter into the exceptional state and reflect on my own thinking. I can never observe my present thinking; I can only subsequently take my experiences of my thinking process as an object for fresh thinking. If I wanted to watch my present thinking, I should have to split myself into two persons, one to think, the other to observe this thinking. But this I cannot do. I can only accomplish it in two separate acts. The thinking to be observed is never that in which I am actually engaged, but another one. Whether, for this purpose, I make observations of my former thinking, or follow the thinking process of another person, or ... assume an imaginary thinking process, is immaterial.
>
> There are two things that are incompatible with one another: productive activity and the simultaneous contemplation of it. This is recognized even in Genesis (I, 31). Here God creates the world in the first six days, and only when it is there is any contemplation of it possible: "And God saw everything that he had made and, behold, it was very good." The same applies to our thinking. It must be there first, if we would observe it. (*The Philosophy of Freedom,* p. 27)

The passage is potentially more difficult for the reader of the *Philosophy,* who hits it early on, than it should be for us. If by "thinking" we mean intentional activity, then the conclusion of the above passage is inevitable.

The argument can be presented in three steps. (1) Consciousness is directional -that is, it is never without an object for consciousness. We are aware of something, something appears for us or to us, whether inward or outward, but we are never simply conscious with an object yet to come. We must be clear about this. Consciousness cannot exist merely in itself, like a thing, but always attends to what is *for* it. There must be a given before we can become conscious, whether it is (a) given passively or (b) given by intentional activity.

(2) Due to the requirement that thinking (intending) can only recognize something akin to itself, a passive given must be intentionally mediated before it gains a form in which it can be observed, while a content given purely by thinking already has a form in which it can be submitted to observation. But to "observe" here means *to observe by thinking* – that is, the object becomes an object of observation by becoming an object of active attention (intention).

(3) In order to observe *this* intention, it must become the object of a second act of intending. The notion that we can passively observe – that is, observe without directed intentional activity, is a misreading and a misunderstanding of mental life. Consciousness is always a moment in which the result of prior intentional activity is submitted to examination by later intentional activity. (Steiner wrote of the moment of observation, above, that once it has made a proposal, *"Thinking* waits for what comes to light of its own accord as a result of restoring the relationship." When reading this we must remember that "thinking" is an activity – its "waiting" advances no further proposal, but it is not *inactive* for that reason. It can observe only by actively attending to what it observes.) We cannot watch the earlier productive activity any more than we could watch ourselves wake up in the morning, and for the same reasons.

As the reader can verify by looking back to the earlier exercises, our own intentional activity was always discovered after the fact, as something we have done, but never as a present object. But we were not for that reason in any doubt of the matter. Our own intentional activity is directly given to us, not because we can watch it happen – who can watch him or herself produce a new idea? – but because when an idea becomes conscious it is clearly meant by us.

Thinking's mode of being – that is, being *meant* or intended – possesses an intelligibility that makes it immediately open to inspection. Steiner continues:

> The reason why it is impossible for us to observe thinking in the actual moment of occurrence, is the very one which makes it possible to know it more immediately and more intimately than any other process in the world. Just because it is our own creation do we know the characteristic features of its course, the manner in which the process takes place. What in all other spheres of observation can be found only indirectly, namely, the relevant context and the relationship between individual objects, is, in the case of thinking, known to us in an absolutely direct way. I do not on the face of it know why, for my observations, thunder follows lightning; but I know directly, from the very content of the two concepts, why my thinking connects the *concept* of thunder with the *concept* of lightning. It does not matter in the least whether I have the right concepts of lightning and thunder. The connection between those concepts is clear to me, and this through the very concepts themselves. *(The Philosophy of Freedom,* pp. 27-8, emphasis mine)

The point is, of course, that he can understand his explanation of events. In his observation lightning is followed by thunder. In his explanation he has identified lightning as cause and thunder as effect, which would certainly explain their connection if true. Whether true to the phenomena or not, however, in the explanation they have been intended as *cause* and *effect* and the relation of these two concepts is transparently clear (through an inspection of their meaning).

The examination of the concepts above, however, can only be performed upon content that is already *given* to our observation, and thus the act of giving is causally prior to that of observing, and both are *actions.* But, adds Steiner, this distinction is not a limitation. Because we give it to ourselves, what has been done in the act is transparently clear through our observation of the results. That the observation takes place after the fact of production does not alter its *content.* So the note in chapter twelve of the *Philosophy* reads:

> That we speak of thoughts (ethical ideas) as objects of
> observation is fully justified. For although during the
> activity of thinking the products of thinking do not appear
> at the same time in the field of observation, they can
> nevertheless become objects of observation afterwards.
> And it is in this way that we have arrived at our
> characterization of action. (p. 170 fn.)

Present thinking may observe past thinking though its products, which is exactly what we have been doing in this long argument. But in the next chapter of the dissertation Steiner will consider the full ramifications of a thought he expresses in the *Philosophy* as follows:

What is impossible with nature – creation before cognition – we achieve with thinking. If we waited, with thinking, until we already understood it, we should never get to that point. We must think resolutely ahead, in order later to arrive by observation at knowledge of what we have done. We ourselves create the object for the observation of thinking. The presence of all other objects has been taken care of without our participation. (p. 32)

Chapter 6:

Theory of Knowledge Free of Assumptions,

and Fichte's Science of Knowledge

As the title of the chapter indicates, the argument here is structured as a critique of Fichte's *Wissenschaftslehre (Science of Knowledge)* perhaps the first attempt to use an awareness of intentionality in a systematic way in philosophic literature. Since Fichte's excesses were almost universally condemned, Steiner does not want any confusion between his own position and that of Fichte. He constructs the argument in such a manner that he can highlight both Fichte's strength and the basis for his error, and pass beyond to his own account of "das Ich" (the "I"), which he has omitted up to this point.

In the preceding analysis the "object of cognition" was assumed to be something other than cognition, but through the same examination cognition itself (and therefore consciousness) became an object of cognition, and was known through its corresponding idea. It is with this idea – *qua* idea – that Steiner begins the new chapter.

> We have now identified the idea of knowledge. This idea is immediately given to human consciousness in so far as it cognizes. Both outer and inner percepts, as well as its own presence are immediately given to the "I," which is the center of consciousness. (It is hardly necessary to say that here "center" is not meant to denote any particular theory of consciousness, but is used merely for the sake of brevity in order to denote the collective physiognomy of consciousness.) The "I" feels a need to discover more in the given than is *immediately* contained in it. In contrast to the given world, a second world – the world of thinking – rises up to meet the I and the I unites the two through its own free decision, realizing what we have identified as the idea of knowledge. (p. 100)

The immediate problem is Steiner's claim that the idea of cognition "is immediately given to human consciousness in so far as it cognizes." The rest of the passage, however, serves as a clarification. We have already seen that when the "I" is faced with a passively received given it becomes active in the production of concepts, mediating the former with the latter and producing by this a result that is both given and meant by the "I," and therefore open to observation.

But since cognition itself is something new in the world, and does not exist before a human being produces it, when the "I" proposes cognition it must advance an intentional proposal that does not belong to any reality already in the world, but to a reality that it will produce through this idea. Arguing that there is a "fundamental difference between the way the concept and the directly given are united within human consciousness to form full reality and the way they are found united in the rest of the world content," Steiner develops the contrast:

> In the rest of the world-picture we must conceive of an original union that is an inherent necessity; an artificial separation occurs only in relation to *knowledge* at the point where cognition begins; cognition then cancels out this separation once more, in accordance with the original nature of the objective world. But in human consciousness the situation is different. Here the union of the two factors of reality depends on the activity of consciousness. In all other objects the separation has no significance for the objects themselves, but only for knowledge. Their union is original and their separation is derived. Cognition separates them only because its nature is such that it cannot grasp their union without having first separated them. (pp. 100)

With his characteristic terseness he then reverses this rule with regard to consciousness itself:

> But the separation of concept and the given reality of consciousness [cognition] is original, and their union is derived; which is why cognition has the nature described here. Just because, for consciousness, idea

and given are necessarily separated, for consciousness
the whole of reality divides into these two factors; and
again, just because consciousness can effect their
union only by its own activity, it can arrive at full
reality only by performing the act of cognition. All
other categories (ideas), prior to being taken up by
cognition, are necessarily united with their
corresponding forms of the given. But the idea of
knowing can be united with its corresponding given
only by the activity of consciousness. Actual
consciousness exists only if it actualizes itself. (p. 100)

The first sentence speaks of an original separation between the
idea of cognition and cognition itself. The explanatory movement
of the rest of the passage develops from the clause "which is why
cognition has the nature described here." For the process of
cognition, concept and given are received separately, and therefore
the "whole of reality" is presented through a union of these two
factors. Since this is the case, however, cognition arrives at reality
by joining the two contents. Two senses of "reality" are contained
here: cognition arrives (1) at a consciousness of reality, and (2) at
the reality of consciousness. But the latter is not part of the world
until the process of cognition makes it so. Thus, while all other
categories are already "united with their corresponding forms of
the given" prior to reception into the cognitive process, the idea of
cognition is united with the reality of cognition only as a result of
the cognitive act. Since this act of cognition creates consciousness,
"Actual *(wirkliches)* consciousness exists only if it actualizes/realizes
(verwirklicht) itself." (Notice that consciousness must produce itself
through an activity which the resulting conscious "I" will identify as i

ts own, after the fact of consciousness. Thus here, as in the later *Philosophy of Freedom,* intentional activity is prior to contemplation, for it is prior to consciousness. Yet this consciousness is, or can be, aware of its self-production, recognizing its own deeds in their products. After all, I find nothing in my consciousness but that which I have grasped by my own activity of understanding.)

The account has now reproduced the "postulate" of chapter four in another form. (You will remember that the postulate was, in Steiner's words: "in the sphere of the given there must be something in relation to which our activity does not hover in emptiness, but where the content of the world itself enters this activity.") When consciousness is actual, the passive given has been contexted by the intentionally given, and we observe the result. That the percept should be mediated with a corresponding concept was not a relation discoverable by cognition, however, for nothing can be cognized before this is decided. When the "I" intends this unity (of percept and concept), it cannot be guided by the demands of a previous given, but is actually *originating* the demand that the given be so mediated.

In Steiner's description, the "I" "feels a need to discover more in the given than is immediately contained in it." Prior to "the given reality of cognition," the "I" responds to its own need, therefore, by designing a mode of action that will satisfy the need: prior to the existence of cognition the "I" must create cognition (and therefore consciousness). Of course, the thinking self is not conscious when it does this. As we heard Steiner remark above, "If we waited, with thinking, until we already understood it, we should never get to that point. We must think resolutely ahead, in order later to arrive by observation at a knowledge of what we have done" *(The Philosophy of Freedom,* p. 32). The self must act in such a manner that cognition will result, and thus must intend the idea of cognition as the form of the action. Since this idea corresponds to no reality other than the one it will create, the idea is a "decree" of the "I" rather than something demanded by another source.

Now that the new subject, the relation of intentional activity to consciousness itself, is visible, Steiner will turn to Fichte. The chapter was obviously written to an audience familiar with Fichte and the problems of his text. Although Fichte is little read today, Steiner's quotations and commentary make the relation to his own work quite clear. The sentence following the indented quotation above reads: "I believe that I have now cleared the ground sufficiently to enable us to understand Fichte's *Science of Knowledge* through recognition of the fundamental mistake contained in it." Focusing on this "mistake" Steiner expands:

> He felt that what I have called the second step in the
> theory of knowledge, and which I formulated as a
> postulate, must be actively performed by the "I."
> This can be seen, for example, from these words:
> "The science of knowledge ... is built up ... through
> a determination of freedom; which freedom, in the
> science of knowledge, is particularly determined: to
> become conscious of the general manner of acting
> of the intelligence ..." What does Fichte mean by
> the "acting of intelligence" if we express in clear
> concepts what he dimly felt? Nothing other than the
> realization of the idea of cognition in consciousness.
> Had Fichte been clear about this he would have

formulated the above principle as follows: A science of knowledge has the task of bringing to consciousness the act of cognition, in so far as it is still an unconscious activity of the "I": it must show that to objectify the idea of cognition is a necessary deed of the "I." (p. 101)

Again, the "postulate" of chapter four was that cognitive activity must begin with something akin to itself – where it "finds itself active in the very essence of the given." Even so the activity of cognition begins by intending conceptual content to mediate the directly given. Since this activity is done for the sake of an observable result, the "postulate" was the first expression of the idea of cognition. This is what Fichte "dimly" intuits as the "acting of intelligence." But he never grasps the idea itself, and thus cannot show that "the objectification of the idea of cognition is a necessary deed of the "I." Since in this same chapter Steiner speaks of the unification of ideas with their corresponding given as an "objectification" *(Objectivierung)* of the ideas, the objectification of the idea of cognition can only be the production of the actuality of cognition. After all, the idea has no necessary connection to anything before cognition becomes actual, and its actualization is that of consciousness.

Fichte did not study cognition itself, focusing entirely on the free self-determination of the "I." The "I," he insists, "posits its own existence." Steiner accepts the notion of self-determination but then points out that Fichte has not thought this claim through. Fichte begins from the intuited truth that "the 'I' can begin to be active only through an absolute original decision."

But for Fichte it is impossible to find the actual content of the original activity posited by the "I." He had nothing toward which this activity could be directed or by which it could be determined. The "I" is to do something, but *what* is it to do? Fichte did not formulate the concept of knowledge that the "I" is to realize, and in consequence he strove in vain to identify any further activity of the "I" beyond the original deed. (p. 101)

If the freedom of the originating deed of the idea is to mean something, it must possess specific content.

Even if the "I" is free insofar as its own activity is concerned, nevertheless the "I" cannot but posit something. It cannot posit "activity, as such, by itself," but only a definite activity ... Unless the "I" sets to work on something given which it posits, it can do "nothing," and therefore cannot posit either. Fichte's own principle actually shows this: the "I" posits its existence. Existence is a category. This means we have arrived at our principle: the activity of the "I" is to posit, by a free decision, the concepts and ideas of the given. Fichte arrives at this conclusion only because he unconsciously set out to prove that the "I" "exists." Had he worked out the concept of cognition, he would have arrived at the true starting point for a theory of knowledge, namely: the "I" posits cognition. (p. 103)

Steiner's criticisms actually reveal how close Fichte came to important discoveries. Fichte argues, for example, that one must

> Attend to yourself: turn your attention away from everything that surrounds you and toward your inner life; this is the demand that philosophy makes on its disciple. Our concern is not with anything that lies outside, but only with yourself. (pp. 103-104)

Because

> This science presupposes a completely new inner sense organ, through which a new world is revealed which does not exist for the ordinary man at all. (p. 104)

Fichte's "action of intelligence" is that of "positing" *(setzen)* existence, and only that which has been posited by *"das Ich"* can exist for the self. His term has since been replaced by "intending," but the meaning is very much the same. The "new inner sense organ" is the awareness through which we can observe this positing activity, and every writer who has struggled to communicate something of the nature of intentional activity has had to find the equivalent of this passage.

(Of course, the warning that this work requires the development of such a sense organ serves to prepare his audience for a shift in focus that will alter the meanings of language. As we have seen, Steiner had the same problem. His epistemological account is not an argument in the ordinary sense of the word, but actually a description of intentional activity. The difficulty encountered in his presentation is brought about by the dependence of his language, for its meaning, on the inner experience of intentionality. Without this experience the intelligibility of the text fails. For those who have taken possession of the experience, or have developed the new sense, language has a new content because we become aware of what would otherwise be invisible to us.)

But Fichte was trained, as it were, by reading Kant, and although he has discovered his own intentional activity, he misses the role of the percept and assumes that the self's positing is always unconditioned – that is, free. Unfortunately that would mean that the only ground of reality was the activity of the "I," which must then appear to create the world out of itself. So Steiner comments:

> In self-observation the activity of the "I" is actually seen, not one-sidedly turned in a particular direction, not as merely positing existence, but revealing many aspects of itself as it strives to grasp directly the world-content in thinking. Self-observation reveals the "I" engaged in the activity of building up the world picture by combining the given with concepts. For someone who has not elaborated the above considerations for himself, however, and who therefore does not know that the "I" only arrives at the full content of reality when it approaches the given with its thought-forms – for him the process of knowledge appears to consist of spinning the world out of the "I" itself. This is why Fichte sees the world-picture more and more as a construction of the "I." He emphasizes ever more strongly that it is essential for the science of knowledge to awaken the faculty for watching the "I" while it constructs the world. He who is able to do this appears to Fichte to be at a higher stage of knowledge than someone who can see only the construction, only the finished

product ... Ordinary consciousness sees only what is posited (*was gesetzt* ist) what is in some way or other determined. It lacks insight into the antecedent, into the ground – that is, why something is posited in just the way it is, and not otherwise. To secure knowledge of these antecedents is, for Fichte, the task of a completely new sense organ. (p. 104)

In a reversal of the usual criticisms, Fichte's error arises not from his radical turn toward the activity of the "I" but because the turn was not radical enough. Fichte's critics fault him for deriving the world from his own subjectivity – Steiner, for supposing, along with his critics, that the content of intentional activity is determined only by the subjective self. The same remarks could be leveled at many of the modern critics of phenomenology and some of its practitioners. One needs, as Fichte argues, a "completely new sense organ" to approach the problem, but it was not Fichte who measured the ground:

> No matter from what aspect Fichte is considered, we shall find that his line of thought gains power and life when we think of the activity of the "I," which he presents as gray and empty of content, as filled and organized by what we have called the process of cognition. (p. 105)

In the next paragraph Steiner summarizes the import of the chapter, showing the actual advance in presentation his examination of Fichte has allowed:

> The fact that the "I" is freely able to become active in

itself makes it possible for it to produce the category of cognition through self-determination; in the rest of the world, by objective necessity the categories are connected with the given corresponding to them. It must be the task of ethics and metaphysics to investigate the nature of this free self-determination on the basis of this theory of knowledge. These sciences will also have to investigate whether the "I" can objectify ideas other than those of cognition. The present discussion shows that the "I" is free when it cognizes, when it objectifies the ideas of cognition. For when the directly given and the thought-form belonging to it are united by the "I" in the process of cognition, then the union of these two elements of reality – which otherwise would remain forever separated in consciousness – can only take place though a free act. (p. 105)

In the "rest of the world" things are already determined by the relations that make them what they are, but to become what it is — a cognizer – the "I" must first produce the idea of cognition through an activity that is also a self-determination . And now for the first time Steiner can allow the argument to pass on to the goals that Fichte had in mind, but which were impossible for Fichte due to his failure to grasp cognition. "It must be the task of ethics and metaphysics to investigate the nature of this free self-determination," which sciences "will also have to discuss whether the "I" is able to objectify ideas other than those of cognition." Are there ideas "other than those of cognition" through which the "I" may also be said to self-determine? By asking that metaphysics and ethics investigate the question, Steiner has proposed that there are, and will take up the investigation himself in the "Practical Conclusion" (chapter 8).

The concluding paragraphs, beginning with the remark, "Our discussion sheds a completely new light on critical idealism" (p. 106) summarize the results of the chapter in two points. First, "no idealism can derive from the 'I' that form of the world-content which is here described as the directly given." (In order to emphasize the closure of this question Steiner reminds the reader of Hume's discussion of the missing hue in a graded series of colors and shows that his treatment has provided a definitive answer: "One need only consider that if all colors were given us with the exception of one single shade, even then we could not begin to provide that shade from the 'I' alone.") The second point is the complement to this discussion of given particularity: "The essential What of the given is posited by the 'I' only through the 'I' itself." (p. 106)

Expanding on the last point, Steiner remarks:

> The "I" would have no occasion to posit within itself the nature of something given did it not first find itself confronted by a completely undetermined given. Therefore what is posited by the "I" as the essence (*Wesen*) of the world is not posited without the "I" but through it.
>
> The true shape is not the first in which reality comes before the "I," but the shape that the "I" gives it ... It is the shape in which the world is first given, rather than the shape it attains through theorizing activity, that is subjective.

The argument is a rather daring completion of Fichte's thrust – his notion that somehow everything came from the "I." But the

"I" does not create reality because it does not create particularity. It does, however, create the intelligibility of the phenomenal world, which intelligibility it posits "in itself." One cannot escape the suggestion that in looking at an intelligible world we are also viewing a transformed "I-ness" – or the given in the form of the "I."

Chapter Seven:
Conclusion in Terms of the Theory of Knowledge

This chapter reviews the above conclusions and makes the additional argument that the development of a proper idea of cognition is a crucially important step toward transcending "one-sided world-views." The examples given of the latter include dogmatism, subjective idealism, skepticism, empiricism, and rationalism, a list that foreshadows the longer discussions of *The Philosophy of Freedom.* Each outlook is presented as the result of the same error:

> One-sidedness, as a rule, results from the fact that an inquiry approached this or that object of cognition rather than the process of cognition itself. (p. 108)

The rest of the paragraph will give such an account of the views mentioned:

> Our discussion has shown that neither the "thing-in-itself" of dogmatism, nor the "I" of subjective idealism, can be fundamental, for the mutual relationship of these must first be determined by

98

thinking. One cannot derive either of these from the other – thinking must determine both according to their character and relation. Skepticism must relinquish its doubt of the possibility of knowledge, for there is no sense in doubting the "given" since it is untouched by all predicates. But should the skeptic doubt that cognitive activity could approach things, this can only be done through a thinking consideration, which contradicts the position. The attempt to ground doubt through thinking implies that thinking has the power to support conviction. Finally our theory of knowledge transcends both one-sided empiricism and one-sided rationalism by uniting them on a higher level. In this manner justice is done to both. Empiricism is justified by showing that as far as content is concerned, knowledge of the given is attained only by direct contact with the given. Rationalism also finds justification in this approach in that thinking is shown to be the necessary and only mediator of knowledge. (pp. 108)

After a brief review of the related work of A. E. Biedermann, Steiner concludes:

We believe that we have shown that all conflicts between world views result from the attempt to gain knowledge of something objective (thin, "I," consciousness, etc.) without having first gained sufficient understanding of that which alone can elucidate all knowledge: *the nature of knowledge itself.* (p. 109)

The entire argument of this chapter arises as a reflection on the most penetrating insight of Steiner's account: that intentional activity must precede the acquisition of an object of consciousness. Once this is understood, it becomes obvious that a theory of knowledge that begins from such an object must distort the resulting picture; thus the list of "corrections" above.

Of course, the correction to methodology arising from this grasp of cognition is still to be worked out, and the text offers no account of the type of scientific investigation that would follow from a grasp of thinking that is primarily intentional rather than propositional. As one sees from his work on Goethe's science and his own lectures on scientific subjects, however, Steiner was quite aware that his epistemology would alter the nature of scientific investigation.

Chapter Eight: Practical Conclusion

This chapter is necessarily the most condensed for it recognizes possibilities nascent in the preceding discussion. Thus the first sentence restates the task of the work:

> The aim of the preceding discussion has been to throw light on the relationship between our cognizing personality and the objective world. (p. 110)

The next two paragraphs restate the conclusion:

> Our discussion has shown that the most inward

essence of the world lives in our knowledge. The lawful harmony that governs the cosmos comes to manifestation in human cognition.

It is part of the human task to bring into the sphere of appearance those fundamental laws that govern all manifest being, but would otherwise not come into manifestation themselves. It is the essence of our knowing that the world-ground, which is never to be found as such in objective reality, is presented in it. Our cognition – to speak pictorially – is a continuous growing into the world-ground. (p. 110)

The equation of cognition with the production of appearance allows the statement to generalize upon three distinct revelations: the experience of the concept within human subjectivity, the original production and subsequent metamorphosis of phenomena toward increasing intelligibility, and finally, art – the production of aesthetically enhanced phenomena. All these are now seen in terms of bringing fundamental laws to manifestation, an interpretation that stands in direct opposition to Kantian and neo-Kantian accounts. The implied resolution of aesthetics is particularly surprising, since it is based on cognition, an activity excluded from aesthetic experience by Hume, Kant, and Croce. Steiner does not turn toward these rich implications however, for he has another concern in mind.

The chapter is the "practical" conclusion and, since Kant's second critique, "practical reason" has meant moral reason. Steiner will now make good on his subtitle -

"Introduction for a Philosophy of Freedom" – arguing that even as this account of cognition must redefine epistemology and aesthetics, so it must also be definitive for ethics. The discussion here is equally surprising, since it suggests that our cognitive powers can also be the basis of ethics.

Most ethical arguments attempt to discover the content of ethical law; they argue in order to justify a claim of what we ought to do. Steiner pays no attention to this project, turning instead to the ground of ethical responsibility – that, to what authority do we owe this responsibility?

The argument begins with a generalization that follows from the previous chapters.

> The human being is therefore called upon to bring into a realm on manifest reality those fundamental laws of the world which do indeed govern all existence, but which otherwise never come to existence. That is the nature of knowing: that in the world-ground, which is never found in objective reality, presents itself. Our knowing activity – expressed pictorially – is continuous living into the ground of the world. (p. 93)

But the next sentence reads:

> Such a conviction must also shed light on the way we take up practical life.

If human beings are governed by moral laws, then these laws will be part of the general lawfulness of the world, and will have to be brought to manifestation in the same manner as other laws. But the result of the knowledge so produced is quite different from the result of a knowledge of outer nature.

> Whenever something takes place in the universe we can distinguish a twofold character: the outer course the event follows in space and time, and the inner lawfulness.
>
> To comprehend such a law in the sphere of human conduct is simply a special instance of cognition. Thus the insight we have gained concerning the nature of cognation must be useful here as well. To know oneself as a behaving personality means to know the law corresponding to one's behavior – that is, to possess the moral concepts and ideals as knowledge. If we recognize these laws, then our actions are our doing. (p. 94)

What is being known in the passage is not only oneself, but oneself "as a behaving personality," the sort of knowledge that would tell us what is characteristic of a personality, but this time focused upon ourselves. The argument is merely sketched, and since the text offers no help in this task of knowing, it may not immediately appeal to the understanding. In particular, the sense of a doing that is our own needs clarification. The section continues:

> In such instances the law is not something given, lying outside the object in which the event appears, but is the content of the object itself engaged in living activity. The object in this case is

our own "I." If the "I" has really penetrated its deed with full insight, in conformity with its nature, then it also feels itself to be master. As long as this is not the case, the laws ruling the deed confront us as something foreign, they rule us; what we do is done under the compulsion they exert over us. If they are transformed from being a foreign entity into a deed originating completely within our own I, all compulsion ceases. That which compelled us has become our own being ... To recognize the laws of one's deeds means to become conscious of one's own freedom. Thus the process of cognition is the process of development toward freedom. (pp. 94-95)

That the *Erkenntnisprozess* (process of cognition) can be identified with the *Entwicklungsprozess zur Freiheit* (process of development toward freedom) is a somewhat surprising point, and that very sense of surprise can be a guide to the insight. Upon reflection, the conclusion can only surprise due to its contrast with the effect of cognition directed at something other than the thinker. Cognitive activity, in the case of the not-self, does not alter the nature of the object of cognition but produces only the conditions under which that nature can become evident to consciousness. But the effect of cognition is different with regard to the self. Here something that would not otherwise exist – consciousness itself – is created.

If consciousness must create itself through the invention of cognition, then the laws of this cognition actually proceed from the nature of the conscious self, and this creation is a free act. But while this is not yet known, the conscious self cannot experience any freedom in these laws, for they appear to be the result of external necessity. An observation of the nature of thinking, however, can reveal that these laws are our own. It is to this example that Steiner points in chapter six when speaking of the further tasks implied by his epistemology:

> The fact that the "I" is freely able to become active in itself makes it possible for it to produce the category of cognition through self-determination; in the rest of the world, by objective necessity the categories are connected with the given corresponding to them. It must be the task of ethics and metaphysics to investigate the nature of this free self-determination on the basis of this theory of knowledge. These sciences will also have to investigate whether the "I" can objectify ideas other than those of cognition. That the objectification of the idea of cognition occurs through freedom, however, is already clear from the above discussion. For when the directly given and the thought-form belonging to it are united by the "I" in the process of cognition, the union of these two elements of reality – which otherwise would remain forever separated in consciousness – can only take place though a free act. (p. 85)

The act of cognition makes the not-self intelligible and the self conscious. It is a free act, for to be active in this manner the "I" must create the category of cognition through self-determination. Yet consciousness must still grasp itself, and unless the "I" also grasps its own self-determination, its role as creator of the idea of cognition remains hidden from it. A conscious self who does not know his or her own freedom is no more free than a dreamer who dreams of confinement in prison. External objects are what they are whether or not we grasp them, and the unconscious self is obviously beyond our grasp, but the self-conscious self can only *be* what it can *know* of itself. The "I" must realize the idea of its own cognitive activity in order to realize its freedom – to grasp that the "laws of logic" are its own intentions, and knowledge its own creation.

But the passage above adds that ethics and metaphysics will have to investigate whether the "I" can objectify ideas other than those of cognition. Now we must reflect that the "I" was not free because it cognized – because it knew – but because it brought this about through self-determination. If the "I" can objectify ideas other than those of cognition, this will also take place through self-determination, for nothing in the world could demand it.

Those who are able to work through the idea of cognition to an observation of cognition discover – if at first only fleetingly – that the task of thinking is not thrust upon us by an enigmatic universe, but is our own free creation, and the manifest intelligibility of the world is a human product. Since this is the case, all problems for cognition have been invented by cognition itself, and contain only those determinations that arise out of our own world of ideas. Consider how well Steiner's remarks about moral freedom also fit cognition:

> In such instances the law is not something given, lying outside the object in which the event appears, but is the content of the object itself engaged in living activity. The object in this case is our own "I." If the "I" has really penetrated its deed with full insight, in conformity with its nature, then it also feels itself to be master. (p. 94)

Cognition is a task we give ourselves; in it we are free. It is this sense of freedom that, when gained, must be our guide to ethical freedom. Here, the ideas we objectify determine the nature of the personality, and therefore govern the actions of the personality in the world. "To know oneself as a behaving personality" is to grasp what else, besides thinking, follows from the nature of this individual "I."

Bibliography

Steiner, Rudolf (1988/1883-97). *Goethean Science,* translated by William Lindeman. Spring Valley, NY: Mercury Press.

Steiner, Rudolf (2008/1886). *Goethe's Theory of Knowledge: An Outline of the Epistemology of His Worldview.* Great Barrington, MA: SteinerBooks.

Steiner, Rudolf (1979/1894). *The Philosophy of Freedom,* translated by Michael Wilson. London: Rudolf Steiner Press. Also published in English under the titles *Philosophy of Spiritual Activity* and *Intuitive Thinking as a Spiritual Path.*

Dedicated with warmth and reverence to

EDUARD VON HARTMANN

by the author

PREFACE TO THE EDITION OF 1892

Present day philosophy suffers from an unhealthy faith in Kant.* This essay is intended to be a contribution toward overcoming this. It would be sacrilegious to belittle this man's lasting contributions to the development of German philosophy and science. But the time has come to recognize that the foundation for a truly satisfying view of the world and of life can be laid only by adopting a position which contrasts strongly with Kant's. What did he achieve? He showed that the foundation of things lying beyond the world of our senses and our reason, and which his predecessors sought to find by means of falsely understood conceptual stereotypes, is inaccessible to our faculty of knowledge. From this he concluded that our scientific efforts must be limited to what is within reach of experience, and that we cannot attain knowledge of the supersensible foundation, of the "thing-in-itself." But suppose the "thing-in-itself" and a transcendent ultimate foundation of things are nothing but illusions! It is easy to see that this is the case. It is an instinctive urge, inseparable from human nature, to search for the fundamental nature of things and their ultimate principles. This is the basis of all scientific activity. There is, however, not the slightest reason for seeking the foundation of things *outside* the given physical and spiritual world, as long as a comprehensive investigation of this world does not lead to the discovery of elements *within* it that clearly point to an influence coming from beyond it.

The aim of this essay is to show that everything necessary to explain and account for the world is within the reach of our thinking. The assumption that there are principles which belong to our world, but lying outside it, is revealed as the prejudice of an outdated philosophy living in vain and illusory dogmas. Kant himself would have had to come to this conclusion had he really investigated the powers inherent in our thinking. Instead of this, he showed in the most complicated way that we cannot reach the ultimate principles existing beyond our direct experience, because of the way our faculty of knowledge functions. There is, however, no rational reason for transferring these principles into another world. Kant did indeed refute "dogmatic" philosophy, but he put nothing in its place. This is why Kant was opposed by the German philosophy which followed. Fichte,* Schelling* and Hegel* did not worry in the least about the limits to cognition erected by Kant, but sought the ultimate principles *within* the world accessible to human reason. Even Schopenhauer,* though he maintained that the conclusions of Kant's criticism of reason were eternal and irrefutable truths, found himself compelled to search for the ultimate cause along paths very different from those of Kant. The mistake of these thinkers was that they sought knowledge of the highest truths without having first laid a foundation by investigating the nature of knowledge itself. This is why the imposing edifice of thought erected by Fichte, Schelling and Hegel stands there, so to speak, without foundations. This had a bad effect on the direction taken by the thought of these philosophers. Because they did not understand the significance of the sphere of pure ideas and its relationship to the realm of sense-perceptions, they added mistake to mistake, one-sidedness to one-sidedness. It is no wonder that their all too daring systems could not withstand the fierce opposition of an epoch so ill-disposed toward philosophy; consequently, along with the errors much of real value in their thought was mercilessly swept away.

The aim of the following inquiry is to remedy the lack described above. Unlike Kant, the purpose here is not to show what our faculty of knowledge *cannot* do, but rather to show what it is really able to achieve.

The outcome of what follows is that truth is not, as is usually assumed, an ideal reflection of something real, but is a product of the human spirit, created by an activity which is *free*; this product would exist nowhere if we did not create it ourselves. The object of knowledge is not to *repeat* in conceptual form something which already exists, but rather to *create* a completely new sphere, which when combined with the world given to our senses constitutes complete reality. Thus man's highest activity, his spiritual creativeness, is an organic part of the universal world-process. The world-process would not be considered a complete, enclosed totality without this activity. Man is not a an idle onlooker in relation to world events, merely repeating in mental pictures cosmic events taking place without his participation; he is the active co-creator of the world-process, and cognition is the most perfect link in the organism of the universe.

This insight has the most significant consequences for the laws that underlie our deeds, that is, our moral ideals; these, too, are to be considered not as copies of something existing outside us, but as being present solely *within* us. This also means rejecting the "categorical imperative," an external power whose commandments we have to accept as moral laws, comparable to a voice from the Beyond that tells us what to do or leave undone. Our moral ideals are our own free creations. We have to fulfill only what we ourselves lay down as our standard of conduct. Thus the insight that truth is the outcome of a free deed also establishes a philosophy of morality, the foundation of which is the completely *free personality.*

These sentences are valid, of course, only for that part of our actions whose laws we penetrate ideally in complete understanding. As long as we are not clear about the motives — either natural or conceptual — for our conduct, we shall experience our motives as something compelling us from outside, even though someone on a higher level of spiritual development could recognize the extent to which our motives originated within our own individuality. Every time we succeed in penetrating a motive with clear understanding, we win a victory in the realm of freedom.

The reader will come to see in detail how this view — especially in its epistemological aspects — is related to that of the most significant philosophical work of our time, the worldview of Eduard von Hartmann.*

This essay constitutes a prologue to *The Philosophy of* Freedom,* a work which will appear shortly.

Clearly, the ultimate goal of all knowledge is to enhance the value of human existence. He who does not consider this to be his ultimate goal, only works as he learned from those who taught him; he "investigates" because that happens to be what he has learned to do. He can never be called "an independent thinker."

The true value of learning lies in the philosophical demonstration of the significance of its results for humanity. It is my aim to contribute to this. But perhaps modern science does not ask for justification! If so, two things are certain. first, that I shall have written a superfluous work; second, that modern scholars are striving in vain, and do not know their own aims.

In concluding this preface, I cannot omit a personal remark. Until now, I have always presented my philosophical views in connection with Goethe's worldview. I was first introduced to this by my revered teacher, Karl Julius Schroer* who, in my view, reached such heights as a scholar of Goethe's work because he always looked beyond the particular to the *Idea*.

In this work, however, I hope to have shown that the edifice of my thought rests upon its own foundation, and need not be derived from Goethe's worldview. My thoughts, as here set forth, and as they will be further amplified in *The Philosophy of Freedom*, have been developed over many years. And it is with a feeling of deep gratitude that I here acknowledge how the friendliness of the Specht family in Vienna, while I was engaged in the education of their children,* provided me with an ideal environment for developing these ideas; to this should be added that I owe the final shape of many thoughts now to be found in my *Philosophy of Freedom* to the stimulating talks with my deeply appreciated friend, Rosa Mayreder* in Vienna; her own literary works, which spring from a sensitive, noble, artistic nature, presumably will soon be published.

Written in Vienna in the beginning of December 1891.

Dr. Rudolf Steiner

INTRODUCTION

The object of the following discussion is to analyze the act of cognition and reduce it to its fundamental elements, in order to enable us to formulate the problem of knowledge correctly and to indicate a way to its solution. The discussion shows, through critical analysis, that no theory of knowledge based on Kant's line of thought can lead to a solution of the problems involved. However, it must be acknowledged that Volkelt's work,[1] with its thorough examination of the concept of "experience" provided a foundation without which my attempt to define precisely the concept of the "given" would have been very much more difficult. It is hoped in this essay to lay a foundation for overcoming the subjectivism inherent in all theories of knowledge based on Kant's philosophy. Indeed, I believe I have achieved this by showing that the subjective form in which the picture of the world presents itself to us in the act of cognition — prior to any scientific explanation of it — is merely a necessary transitional stage which is overcome in the very process of knowledge. In fact the experience which positivism and neo-Kantianism advance as the one and only certainty is just the most subjective one of all. By showing this, the foundation is also laid for objective idealism, which is a necessary consequence of a properly understood theory of knowledge. This objective idealism differs from Hegel's metaphysical, absolute idealism, in that it seeks the reason for the division of reality into *given existence* and *concept* in the cognizing subject itself; and holds that this division is resolved, not in an objective world-dialectic but in the subjective process of cognition. I have already advanced this viewpoint in *Goethe's*

---

[1] *Erfahrung und Denken: Kritische Grundlegung der Erkenntnistheorie (Experience and Thinking: The Critical Foundations of Epistemology*, by Johannes Volkelt, Hamburg und Leipzig, 1886.

Theory of Knowledge,* but my method of inquiry was a different one, nor did I analyze the basic elements in the act of cognition as will be done here.

A list of the more recent literary works which are relevant is given below. It includes not only those works which have a direct bearing on this essay, but also all those which deal with related problems. No specific reference is made to the works of the earlier classical philosophers.

The following are concerned with epistemology in general:

R. Avenarius, *Philosophie als Denken der Welt gemäss dem Prinzip des kleinsten Kraftsmasses, usw. (Philosophy as World-Thinking According to the Principle of the Smallest Energy-Mass, etc.)*, Leipzig, 1876.

_____, *Kritik, der reinen Erfahrung (Critique of Pure Experience)*, Vol. I, Leipzig, 1888.

J. F. A. Bahnsen, *Der Widerspruch im Wissen und Wesen der Welt (The Contradiction in Knowledge and Essence of the World)*, Vol. I, Leipzig, 1882.

J. Baumann, *Philosophie als Orientierung über die Welt (Philosophy as Orientation about the World)*, Leipzig, 1872.

J. S. Beck, *Einzig möglicher Standpunkt, aus welchem die kritische Philosophie beurteilt werden muss (The Only Correct Point of View from which Critical Philosophy Should be Judged)*, Riga, 1796.

Friedrich Ed. Benecke, *System der Metaphysik und Religionsphilosophie, usw. (System of Metaphysics and Philosophy of Religion, etc.)*, Berlin, 1839.

Julius Bergmann, *Sein und Erkennen, usw. (Existence and Cognition, etc.)*, Berlin, 1880.

A. E. Biedermann, *Christliche Dogmatik (Christian Dogmatics)*, 2nd Edition, Berlin, 1884-5.

H. Cohen, *Kants Theorie der Erfahrung (Kant's Theory of Experience)*, Berlin, 1871.

P. Deussen, *Die Elemente der Metaphysik (The Elements of Metaphysics)*, 2nd Edition, Leipzig, 1890.

W. Dilthey, *Einleitung in die Geisteswissenschaften, usw. (Introduction to the Spiritual Sciences, etc.)*, Leipzig, 1883. — Especially the introductory chapters dealing with the interrelation of the theory of cognition and the other sciences. — Further references in works by the same author:

Beiträge zur Lösung der Frage von Ursprung unseres Glaubens an die Realität der Aussenwelt und seinem Recht; Sitzungsberichte der Kgl. Preuss. Akademic der Wissenschaften zu Berlin (Contributions to the Solution of Our Belief in the Reality of the Outer World and its Justification. Reports of Meetings of the Royal Prussian Academy of Sciences in Berlin), Berlin, 1890, p. 977.

A. Dorner, *Das menschliche Erkennen usw. (Human Cognition, etc.)*, Berlin, 1887.

E. Dreher, *Über Wahrnehmung und Denken (On Perception and Thinking)*, Berlin, 1878.

G. Engel, *Sein und Denken (Existence and Thinking)*, Berlin, 1889.

W. Enoch, *Der Begriff der Wahrnehmung (The Concept of Perception)*, Hamburg, 1890.

B. Erdmann, *Kants Kriticismus in der esten und zweiten Auflage seiner Kritik der reinen Vernunft (Kant's Criticism in the First and Second Editions of his* Critique of Pure Reason*)*, Leipzig, 1878.

F. v. Feldegg, *Das Gefühl als Fundament der Weltordnung (Feeling as Fundament of Universal Order)*, Vienna, 1890.

E. L. Fischer, *Die Grundfragen der Erkenntnistheorie (The Basic Questions of the Epistemology)*, Mainz, 1887

K. Fischer, *System der Logik und Metaphysik oder Wissenschaftslehre (System of Logic and Metaphysics, or Theory of Science)*, 2nd Edition, Heidelberg, 1865.

_____, *Geschichte der neueren Philosophie (History of More Recent Philosophy)*, Mannheim, 1860, especially the parts concerning Kant.

A. Ganser, *Die Wahrheit (Truth)*, Graz, 1890.

C. Göring, *System der kritischen Philosophie (System of Critical Philosophy)*, Leipzig, 1874.

_____, *Über den Begriff der Erfahrung (On the Concept of Experience)*, in *Vierteljahrsschrift für wissenschaftliche Philosophie (Quarterly for Scientific Philosophy)*, Leipzig, 1 (1877), p. 384.

E. Grimm, *Zur Geschichte des Erkenntnisproblems, usw. (Contribution to the History of the Theory of Cognition, etc.)*, Leipzig, 1890.

F. Grung, *Das Problem der Gewissheit (The Problem of Certainty)*, Heidelberg, 1886.

R. Hamerling, *Die Atomistik des Willens (The Atomic Theory of Will)*, Hamburg, 1891.

F. Harms, *Die Philosophie seit Kant (Philosophy since Kant)*, Berlin, 1876.

E. v. Hartmann, *Kritische Grundlegung des transzendentalen Realismus (Critical Foundations of transcendental Realism)*, 2nd Edition, Berlin, 1875.

_____, *J. H. v. Kirchmanns erkenntnistheoretischer Realismus (J. H. v. Kirchmann's Epistemological Realism)*, Berlin, 1875.

_____, *Das Grundproblem der Erkenntnistheorie, usw. (The Fundamental Problem of Epistemology, etc.)*, Leipzig, 1889.

_____, *Kritische Wanderungen durch die Philosophie der Gegenwart (Critical Wanderings through Contemporary Philosophy)*, Leipzig, 1889.

H. L. F. v. Helmholtz, *Die Tatsachen in der Wahrnehmung (The Facts of Perception)*, Berlin, 1879.

G. Heymans, *Die Gesetze und Elemente des wissenschaftlichen Denkens (The Laws and Elements of Scientific Thinking)*, Leyden, 1890.

A. Hölder, *Darstellung der Kantischen Erkenntnistheorie (A Presentation of Kant's Theory of Cognition)*, Tubingen, 1874.

A. Horwicz, *Analyse des Denkens, usw. (Analysis of Thinking, etc.)*, Halle, 1875.

F. H. Jacobi, *David Hume über den Glauben oder Idealismus und Realismus (David Hume on Faith, or Idealism and Realism)*, Breslau, 1787.

M. Kappes, *Der "Common Sense" als Prinzip der Gewissheit in der Philosophie des Schotten Thomas Reid ("Common Sense" as Principle of Certainty in the Philosophy of the Scotsman, Thomas Reid)*, Munich, 1890.

M. Kauffmann, *Fundamente der Erkenntnistheorie und Wissenschaftslehre (Foundations of a Theory of Cognition and Theory of Science)*, Leipzig, 1890.

B. Kerry, *System einer Theorie der Grenzgebiete (System of a Theory of Border-Areas)*, Vienna, 1890.

J. H. v. Kirchmann, *Die Lehre vom Wissen als Einleitung in das Studium philosophischer Werke (The Theory of Knowledge as Introduction to the Study of Philosophical Works)*, Berlin, 1868.

E. Laas, *Die Kausalitat des Ich (The Causality of the I)*, Vierteljahrsschrift für wissenschaftliche Philosophie *(Quarterly for Scientific Philosophy)*, Leipzig, 4 (1880) p. 1 ff., 185ff., 311ff.

_____, *Idealismus und Positivismus (Idealism and Positivism)*, Berlin, 1879.

F. A. Lange, *Geschichte des Materialismus (History of Materialism)*, Iserlohn, 1873-75.

A. v. Leclair, *Beiträge zu einer monistischen Erkenntnistheorie (Studies for a Monistic Theory of Cognition)*, Breslau, 1882.

_____, *Das kategorische Gepräge des Denkens (The Categorical Mark of Thinking)*, Vierteljahrsschrift für wissenschaftliche Philosophie *(Quarterly for Scientific Philosophy)*, Leipzig, 7 (1883), p. 257 ff.

O. Liebmann, *Kant und die Epigonen (Kant and the Epigones)*, Stuttgart, 1865.

_____, *Zur Analysis der Wirklichkeit (On the Analysis of Reality)*, Strassburg, 1880.

_____, *Gedanken und Tatsachen (Thoughts and Facts)*, Strassburg, 1882.

_____, *Die Klimax der Theorien (The Climax of the Theories)*, Strassburg, 1884.

Th. Lipps, *Grundtatsachen des Seelenlebens (The Fundamental Facts of Soul Life)*, Bonn, 1883.

H. R. Lotze, *System der Philosophie, I Teil: Logik (System of Philosophy, Part I: Logic)*, Leipzig, 1874.

J. V. Mayer, *Vom Erkennen (Concerning Cognition)*, Freiburg i. Br., 1885.

A. Meinong, *Hume-Studien (Essays on Hume)*, Vienna, 1877.

J. St. Mill, *System der induktiven und deduktiven Logik (System of Inductive and Deductive Logic)*, 1843; German translation, Braunschweig, 1849.

W Müntz, *Die Grundlagen der Kantschen Erkenntnistheorie (Foundation of Kant's Theory of Knowledge)*, 2nd Edition, Breslau, 1885.

G. Neudecker, *Das Grundproblem der Erkenntnistheorie (Fundamental Problem of the Theory of Cognition)*, Nordlingen, 1881.

F. Paulsen, *Versuch einer Entwicklungsgeschichte der Kantschen Erkenntnistheorie (Study on the History of the Development of the Kantian Theory of Cognition)*, Leipzig, 1875.

J. Rehmke, *Die Welt als Wahrnehmung und Begriff, usw. (The World as Percept and Concept, etc.)*, Berlin, 1880.

Th. Reid, *Untersuchungen über den menschlichen Geist nach Prinzipien des gesunden Menschenverstandes (Inquiry into the Human Mind according to the Principles of Common Sense)*, 1764; German translation, Leipzig, 1782.

A. Riehl, *Der philosophische Kritizismus und seine Bedeutung für die positive Wissenschaft (Philosophical Criticism and its Importance for Positive Science)*, Leipzig, 1887.

J. Rülf, *Wissenschaft des Weltgedankens und der Gedankenwelt, System einer neuen Metaphysik (Science of Cosmic Thought and the Thought-World, A System of a New Metaphysics)*, Leipzig, 1888.

R. v. Schubert-Soldern, *Grundlagen einer Erkenntnistheorie (Fundamentals of a Theory of Cognition)*, Leipzig, 1884.

G. E. Schulze, *Aenesidemus*, Helmstädt, 1792.

W. Schuppe, *Zur voraussetzungslosen Erkenntnistheorie (Contribution to a Theory of Cognition Free of Presuppositions)*, *Philosophische Monatshefte (Philosophical Monthly)*, Berlin, Leipzig, Heidelberg, 1882, Vol. XVIII, Nos. 6 and 7.

R. Seydel, *Logik oder Wissenschaft vom Wissen (Logic, or the Science of Knowledge)*, Leipzig, 1866.

Christoph v. Sigwart, *Logik (Logic)*, Freiburg i. Br., 1878.

A. Stadler, *Die Grundsätze der reinen Erkenntnistheorie in der Kantischen Philosophie (The Axioms of Pure Epistemology in Kantian Philosophy)*, Leipzig, 1876.

H. Taine, *De l'Intelligence (On Intelligence)*, 5th Edition, Paris, 1888.

A. Trendelenburg, *Logische Untersuchungen (Logical Investigations)*, Leipzig, 1862.

F. Ueberweg, *System der Logik (System of Logic)*, 3rd Edition, Bonn, 1882.

H. Vaihinger, *Hartmann, Dühring, und Lange (Hartmann, Dühring, and Lange)*, Iserlohn, 1876.

Th. Varnbühler, *Widerlegung der Kritik der reinen Vernunft (Refutation of the Critique of Pure Reason)*, Leipzig, 1890.

J. Volkelt, *Immanuel Kants Erkenntnistheorie, usw. (Immanuel Kant's Epistemology, etc.)*, Hamburg, 1879.

————, Erfahrung und Denken *(Experience and Thinking)*, Hamburg, 1886.

R. Wahle, *Gehirn und Bewusstsein (Brain and Consciousness)*, Vienna, 1884.

W. Windelband, *Präludien (Preludes)*, Freiburg i. Br., 1884.

————, *Die verschiedenen Phasen der Kantschen Lehre vom "Ding an sich" (The Various Phases of Kant's Theory of the "Thing-in-Itself), Vierteljahrsschrift für wissenschaftliche Philosophie (Quarterly for Scientific Philosophy)*, Leipzig, 1 (1877), p. 229 ff.

J. H. Witte, *Beiträge zur Verständnis Kants (Contributions to the Understanding of Kant)*, Berlin, 1874.

————, Vorstudien zur Erkenntnis des unerfahrbaren Seins *(Preliminary Studies for the Cognition of Non-Experienceable Existence)*, Bonn, 1876.

H. Wolff, *Über den Zusammenhang unserer Vorstellungen mit Dingen ausser uns (On the Correlation of our Perceptions with Things Outside Ourselves)*, Leipzig, 1874.

Joh. Wolff, *Das Bewusstsein und sein Objekt (Consciousness and its Object)*, Berlin, 1889.

W. Wundt, *Logik* (Logic), Vol. I: *Erkenntnislehre (Theory of Cognition)*, Stuttgart, 1880.

The following titles related to Fichte:

F. C. Biedermann, *De Genetica philosophandi ratione et methodo, praesertim Fichtii, Schellingii, Hegelii, Dissertationis particula prima, syntheticam Fichtii methodum exhibens, etc.*, Lipsiae, 1835.

F. Frederichs, *Der Freiheitsbegriff Kants und Fichtes (The Concept of Freedom of Kant and Fichte)*, Berlin, 1886.

O. Gühloff, *Der transcendentale Idealismus (Transcendental Idealism)*, Halle, 1888.

P. P. Hensel, *Über die Beziehung des reinen Ich bei Fichte zur Einheit der Apperception bei Kant (On the Relation between the Pure I in the Works of Fichte and the Unity of Apperception in Kant)*, Freiburg i. Br., 1885.

G. Schwabe, *Fichtes und Schopenhauers Lehre vom Willen mit ihren Consequenzen für Weltbegreifung und Lebensfuhrung (The Theory of Will of Fichte and Schopenhauer and its Consequences for Understanding the World and the Conduct of Life)*, Jena, 1887.

The numerous works published on the occasion of Fichte's Anniversary in 1862 are of course not included here. However, I would, above all, mention the address by Trendelenburg (A. Trendelenburg, *Zur Erinnerung an J. G. Fichte [To the Memory of J. G. Fichte]*, Berlin, 1862), which contains important theoretical viewpoints.

I.
PRELIMINARY REMARKS

Epistemology is the scientific study of what all of the sciences presuppose without examining it: cognition itself. It is thus a philosophical science, fundamental to all other sciences. Only through epistemology can we learn the value and significance of all insight gained through the other sciences. Thus it provides the foundation for all scientific effort. It is obvious that it can fulfill its proper function only by making presuppositions itself, as far as this is possible, about man's faculty of knowledge. This much this much is generally accepted. Nevertheless, when the better-known systems of epistemology are more closely examined it becomes apparent that a whole series of presuppositions are made at the beginning, which cast doubt on the rest of the argument. It is striking that such hidden assumptions are usually made at the outset, when the fundamental problems of epistemology are formulated. But if the essential problems of a science are misstated, the right solution is unlikely to be forthcoming. The history of science shows that whole epochs have suffered from innumerable mistakes that can be traced to the simple fact that certain problems wrongly formulated. To illustrate this, we need not go back as far as Aristotle's physics or Raymond Lull's *Ars Magna*,* there are plenty of more recent examples. For instance, innumerable problems concerning the purpose of rudimentary organs of certain organisms could only be rightly formulated when the condition for doing so had first been created through the discovery of the Biogenetic Law.* While biology was influenced by teleological views, the relevant problems could not be formulated in a way which could lead to a satisfactory answer. For example, what fantastic ideas were entertained concerning the function of the pineal gland in the human brain, as long as the emphasis was on its purpose! Then comparative anatomy threw some light on the matter by asking a different question; instead of asking what the organ was "for," inquiry began as to whether, in man, it might be merely a remnant from a lower level of evolution. Another example: how many physical questions had to be modified after the discovery of the laws of the mechanical equivalent of heat and of conservation of energy!* In short, success in scientific research depends essentially on whether the problems can be formulated rightly. Even though epistemology occupies a very special place as the basis presupposed by the other sciences, nevertheless, successful progress can only be expected when its fundamental problems are correctly formulated.

The discussion which follows aims so to formulate the problem of cognition that in this very formulation it will do full justice to the essential feature of epistemology, namely, the fact that it is a science which must contain no presuppositions. A further aim is to use this philosophical basis for science to throw light on Johann Gottlieb Fichte's philosophy of science.* Why Fichte's attempt in particular to provide an absolutely certain basis for the sciences is linked to the aims of this essay, will become clear in due course.

II.
KANT'S BASIC EPISTEMOLOGICAL QUESTION

Kant is generally considered to be the founder of epistemology in the modern sense. However, the history of philosophy *before* Kant contains a number of investigations which must be considered as more than mere *germs* of such a science. Volkelt points to this in his standard work on epistemology, saying that critical treatments of this science began as early as Locke.* However, discussions which today come under the heading of epistemology can be found as far back as in the philosophy of ancient Greece.[2] Kant then went into every aspect of all the relevant problems, and innumerable thinkers following in his footsteps went over the ground so thoroughly that in his epigones or in Kant are to be found repetitions of all earlier attempts to solve these problems. Thus where a *factual* rather than a *historical* study of epistemology is concerned, there is no danger of omitting anything important if one considers only the period since the appearance of Kant's *Critique of Pure Reason.* All earlier achievements in this field have been repeated since Kant.

Kant's fundamental question concerning epistemology is: *How are synthetical judgments a priori possible?* Let us consider whether or not this question is free of presuppositions. Kant formulates it because he believes that we can arrive at certain, unconditional knowledge only if we can prove the validity of synthetical judgments a priori. He says: "In the solution of the above problem is comprehended at the same time the possibility of the use of pure reason in the foundation and construction of all sciences which contain theoretical knowledge a priori of objects."[3] "Up

---

[2] Volkelt, p. 20.
[3] *Critique of Pure Reason*, p. 61 in the edition of Kirchmann. All subsequent

on the solution of this problem depends the existence or downfall of the science of metaphysics, thus of its very existence."[4]

Is this problem as Kant formulates it, free of all presuppositions? Not at all, for it says that a system of absolute, certain knowledge can be erected only on a foundation of judgments that are synthetical and acquired independently of all experience. Kant calls a judgment "synthetical" where the concept of the predicate brings to the concept of the subject something which lies completely outside the subject — "although it stands in connection with the subject,"[5] by contrast, in analytical judgment, the predicate merely expresses something which is already contained (though hidden) in the subject. It would be out of place here to go into the extremely acute objections made by Johannes Rehmke[6] to this classification of judgments. For our present purpose it will suffice to recognize that we can arrive at true knowledge only through judgments which add one concept to another in such a way that the content of the second was not already contained — at least *for us* — in the first. If, with Kant, we wish to call this category of judgment *synthetical*, then it must be agreed that knowledge in the form of judgment can only be attained when the connection between predicate and subject is synthetical in this sense. But the position is different in regard to the second part of Kant's question, which demands that these judgments must be acquired a priori, i.e., independent of all experience. After all, it is conceivable that such judgments might not exist at all. (We mean hereby of course the mere possibility of thinking such a thing.) A theory of knowledge must leave open, to begin with, the question of whether we can arrive at a judgment

---

references to the *Critique* and to the *Prolegomena* will be to this edition.
[4] *Prolegomena* § 5.
[5] *Critique of Pure Reason*, p. 53 f.
[6] *Die Welt als Wahrnehmung und Begriff (The World as Percept and Concept)*, p.161 f.

solely by means of experience, or by some other means as well. Indeed, to an unprejudiced mind it must seem that for something to be independent of experience in this way is impossible. For whatever object we are concerned to know, we must become aware of it directly and individually, that is, it must become experience. We acquire mathematical judgment too, only through *direct experience* of particular single examples. This is the case even if we regard them, with Otto Liebmann[7] a s rooted in a certain faculty of our consciousness. In this case, we must say: This or that proposition must be valid, for, if its truth were denied, consciousness would be denied *as well*, but we could only grasp its content, as knowledge, through experience in exactly the same way as we experience a process in outer nature. Irrespective of whether the content of such a proposition contains elements which guarantee its absolute validity or whether it is certain for other reasons, the fact remains that we cannot make it our own unless at some stage it becomes experience for us. This is the first objection to Kant's question.

The second consists in the fact that at the beginning of a theoretical investigation of knowledge, one ought not to maintain that no valid and absolute knowledge can be obtained by means of experience. For it is quite conceivable that experience itself could contain some characteristic feature which would guarantee the validity of insight gained by means of it.

Two presuppositions are thus contained in Kant's formulation of the question. One presupposition is that we need other means of gaining knowledge besides experience, and the second is that all knowledge gained through experience is only approximately valid. It does not occur to Kant that these principles need proof, that they are open to doubt. They are prejudices which he simply takes over from dogmatic

---

[7] *Zur Analysis der Wirklichkeit: Gedanken und Tatsachen (On the Analysis of Reality: Thoughts and Facts).*

philosophy and then uses as the basis of his critical investigations. Dogmatic philosophy assumes them to be valid, and simply uses them to arrive at knowledge accordingly; Kant makes the same assumptions and merely inquires under what conditions they are valid. But suppose they are not valid at all? In that case, the edifice of Kant's doctrine has no foundation whatever. All that Kant brings forward in the five paragraphs preceding his actual formulation of the problem, is an attempt to prove that mathematical judgments are synthetical.[8] But the two assumptions discussed above are retained as scientific prejudices. In the "Introduction" to the *Critique of Pure Reason* it is said: "Experience no doubt teaches us that this or that object is constituted in such and such a manner, but not that it could not possibly exist otherwise," and "Experience never exhibits strict and rigorous, but only assumed and comparative universality (by induction)." In paragraph 1 of the *Prolegomena* we find it said: "Firstly, as regards the *sources* of metaphysical knowledge, the very conception of the latter shows that these cannot be empirical. Its principles (under which not merely its axioms, but also its fundamental conceptions are included) must consequently never be derived from experience, since it is not *physical* but *metaphysical* knowledge, i.e., knowledge beyond experience, that is wanted." And finally Kant says in *The Critique of Pure Reason* (p. 58): "Before all, be it observed, that proper mathematical propositions are always judgments *a priori*, and not empirical, because they carry along with them the conception of necessity, which cannot be given by experience. If this be demurred to, it matters not; I will then limit my assertion to *pure* mathematics, the very conception of which implies that it consists of knowledge altogether non-empirical and a priori." No matter where we open the *Critique of Pure Reason*, we find that all the

---

[8] An approach that, if it does not completely contradict the objections by Rob. Zimmermann (*Über Kants mathematisches Vorurteil und dessen Folgen [On Kant's Mathematical Prejudice and Its Consequences]*), nevertheless puts them in question.

investigations pursued in it are based on these dogmatic principles. Cohen[9] and Stadler[10] attempt to prove that Kant has established the a priori nature of mathematical and purely scientific principles. However, all that the *Critique of Pure Reason* attempts to show can be summed up as follows: Mathematics and pure natural science are a priori sciences; from this it follows that the form of all experiences must be inherent in the subject itself. Therefore, the only thing left that is empirically given is the material of sensations. This is built up into a system of experiences, the form of which is inherent in the subject. The formal truths of a priori theories have meaning and significance only as principles which regulate the material of sensation; they make experience possible, but do not go further than experience. However, these formal truths are the synthetical judgment a priori, and they must — as condition necessary for experience — extend as far as experience itself. The *Critique of Pure Reason* does not at all prove that mathematics and pure science are a priori sciences but only establishes their sphere of validity, *pre-supposing* that their truths are acquired independently of experience. Kant, in fact, avoids discussing the question of proof of the a priori sciences in that he simply excludes that section of mathematics (see conclusion of Kant's last statement quoted above) where even in his own opinion the a priori nature is open to doubt; and he limits himself to that section where he believes proof can be inferred from the concepts alone. Even Johannes Volkelt finds that: "Kant starts from the positive assumption that a necessary and universal knowledge exists as an actual fact." He says moreover: These presuppositions which Kant never specifically attempted to prove, are so contrary to a proper critical theory of knowledge that one must seriously

---

[9] *Kants Theorie der Erfahrung (Kant's Theory of Experience)*.
[10] *Die Grundsätze der reinen Erkenntnistheorie in der Kantischen Philosophie (The Axioms of Pure Epistemology in the Kantian Philosophy)*, p. 76 f.

ask oneself whether the *Critique of Pure Reason* is valid as critical epistemology." Volkelt does find that there are good reasons for answering this question affirmatively, but he adds: "The critical conviction of Kant's theory of knowledge is nevertheless seriously disturbed by this dogmatic assumption."[11] It is evident from this that Volkelt, too, finds that the *Critique of Pure Reason* as a theory of knowledge, is not free of presuppositions.

O. Liebmann, Hölder, Windelband, Ueberweg, Ed. v. Hartmann[12] and Kuno Fischer,[13] hold essentially similar views on this point, namely, that Kant bases his whole argument on the *assumption* that knowledge of pure mathematics and natural science is acquired a priori.

That we acquire knowledge independently of all experience, and that the insight gained from experience is of general value only to a limited extent, can only be conclusions derived from some other investigation. These assertions must definitely be preceded by an examination both of the nature of experience and of knowledge.

---

[11] *Erfahrung und Denken (Experience and Thinking)*, p. 21.

[12] Liebmann, *Analysis*, p. 211 f.; Hölder, *Erkenntnistheorie (Epistemology)*, p.14 ff.; Windelband, *Phasen (Phases)*, p. 239; Überweg, *System der Logik (System of Logic)*, p. 380 f.; Hartmann, *Kritische Grundlegung (Critcical Foundation)*, pp. 142-72.

[13] *Geschichte der neueren Philosophie (The History of Modern Philosophy)*, VB, p. 60. With reference to Kuno Fischer, Volkelt errs when he says that it "is not clear in K. Fischer's presentation whether in his opinion presupposed only the psychological factuality of the universal and necessary judgements, or also their objective validity and rightfulness." For at the indicated passage Fischer says that the main difficulty of *The Critique of Pure Reason* is that its "foundations are dependent on certain presuppositions" that one "needs to accept in order for what follows to be valid." These presupposition are for Fischer the fact that "the fact of knowledge" is established and then through analysis the faculty of knowledge "according to which that fact is itself explained."

Examination of experience could lead to the first principle; examination of knowledge, to the second.

In reply to these criticisms of Kant's critique of reason, it could be said that every theory of knowledge must first lead the reader to where the starting point, free of all presuppositions, is to be found. For what we possess as knowledge at any moment in our life is far removed from this point, and we must first be led back to it artificially. In actual fact, it is a necessity for every epistemologist to come to such a purely didactic arrangement concerning the starting point of this science. But this must always be limited merely to showing to what extent the starting point for cognition really is the absolute start; it must be presented in purely self-evident, analytical sentences and, unlike Kant's argument, contain no assertions which will influence the content of the subsequent discussion. It is also incumbent on the epistemologist to show that his starting point is really free of all presuppositions. All this, however, has nothing to do with the nature of the starting point itself, but is quite independent of it and makes no assertions about it. Even when he begins to teach mathematics, the teacher must try to convince the pupil that certain truths are to be understood as axioms. But no one would assert that the *content* of the axioms is made dependent on these preliminary considerations.[14] In exactly the same way the epistemologist must show in his introductory remarks how one can arrive at a starting point free of all presuppositions; yet the actual content of this starting point must be quite independent of these considerations. However, anyone who, like Kant, makes definite, dogmatic assertions at the very outset, is certainly very far from fulfilling these conditions when he introduces his theory of knowledge.

---

[14] In the chapter titled "The Starting Point of Epistemology," I shall show to what extent my discussion fulfils these conditions.

III.
EPISTEMOLOGY SINCE KANT

All propounders of theories of knowledge since Kant have been influenced to a greater or lesser degree by the mistaken way he formulated the problem of knowledge. As a result of his "a priorism" he advanced the view that all objects given to us are our *representations*. Ever since, this view has been made the basic principle and starting point of practically all epistemological systems. The only thing we can establish as an immediate certainty is the principle that we are aware of our representations; this principle has become an almost universally accepted belief of philosophers. As early as 1792 G. E. Schulze maintained in his *Aenesidemus** that all our knowledge consists of mere representations, and that we can never go beyond our representations. Schopenhauer, with a characteristic philosophical fervor, puts forward the view that the enduring achievement of Kantian philosophy is the principle that the world is "my representation." Eduard von Hartmann finds this principle so irrefutable that in his book, *Kritische Grundlegung des transzendentalen Realismus (Critical Foundation of Transcendental Realism)* he assumes that his readers, by critical reflection, have overcome the naive identification of the perceptual picture with the thing-in-itself, that they have convinced themselves of the *absolute diversity* of the subjective-ideal content of consciousness — given as perceptual object through the act of representing — and the thing existing by itself, independent both of the act of representing and of the form of consciousness; in other words, readers who have entirely convinced themselves that the totality of what is given us directly consists of our *representations*.[15] In his final work on epistemology, Eduard von

---

[15] *Kritische Grundlegung (Critical Foundations)*, Preface, p. 10.

Hartmann did attempt to provide a foundation for this view. The validity of this in relation to a theory of knowledge free from presuppositions, will be discussed later. Otto Liebmann claims that the principle: "Consciousness cannot jump beyond itself" must be the inviolable and foremost principle of any science of knowledge.[16] Volkelt is of the opinion that the first and most immediate truth is: "All our knowledge extends, to begin with, only as far as our representations"; he called this the positivist principle of knowledge, and considered a theory of knowledge to be "eminently critical" only if it "considers this principle as the sole stable point from which to begin all philosophizing, and from then on thinks it through consistently."[17] Other philosophers make other assertions the center of epistemology, e.g.: the essential problem is the question of the relation between thinking and existence, as well as the possibility of mediation between them,[18] or again: How does that which exists become conscious? (Rehmke) etc. Kirchmann starts from two epistemological axioms: "the perceived is" and "the contradictory is not."[19] According to E. L. Fischer knowledge consists in the recognition of something *factual* and *real*.[20] He lays down this dogma without proof as does Goring, who maintains something similar: "Knowledge always means recognizing something that exists; this is a fact that neither scepticism nor Kantian criticism can deny."[21] The two latter philosophers simply lay down the law: This they say is knowledge, without questioning by what right this can happen.

Even if these different assertions were correct, or led to a correct formulation of the problem, the place to discuss them is definitely not at

---

[16] *Zur Analysis (On the Analysis)*, p. 28 ff.
[17] *Kants Erkenntnistheorie (Kant's Epistemology)*, § 1.
[18] Dorner, *Das menschliche Erkennen (Human Cognition)*.
[19] *Die Lehre vom Wissen (The Theory of Knowledge)*.
[20] *Grundfragen (Basic Questions)*, p. 385.
[21] *System (System)*, p. 257.

the beginning of a theory of knowledge. *For they all stand as quite specific insights within the sphere of knowledge.* To say that my knowledge extends to begin with only as far as my representations, is to express a quite definite judgment about cognition. In this sentence I add a predicate to the world given to me, namely, its existence in the form of representation. But how do I know, *prior to all knowledge*, that the things given to me are *representations?*

Thus this principle ought not to be placed at the foundation of a theory of knowledge; that this is true is most easily appreciated by tracing the line of thought that leads up to it. This principle has become in effect a part of the whole modern scientific consciousness. The considerations which have led to it are to be found rather systematically and comprehensively summarized in Part I of Eduard von Hartmann's book, *Das Grundproblem der Erkenntnistheorie (The Fundamental Problem of Epistemology).* What is advanced there can thus serve as a kind of guide when discussing the reasons that led to the above assumption.

These reasons are physical, psycho-physical, physiological, as well as philosophical.

The physicist who observes phenomena that occur in our environment when, for instance, we perceive a sound, is led to conclude that these phenomena have not the slightest resemblance to what we directly perceive as sound. Out there in the space surrounding us, nothing is to be found except vibrations of material bodies and of air. It is concluded from this that what we ordinarily call sound or tone is solely a subjective reaction of our organism to those wave-like movements. Likewise it is found that light, color and heat are something purely subjective. The phenomena of color-diffraction, refraction, interference and polarization show that these sensations correspond to certain transverse vibrations in external space, which, so it is thought, must be ascribed partly to material bodies, partly to an infinitely fine elastic substance, the ether. Furthermore, because of certain physical phenomena, the physicist finds herself compelled to abandon the belief in the continuity of objects in space, and to analyze them into systems of minute particles (molecules, atoms) the size of which, in relation to the distance between them, is immeasurably small. Thus he concludes that material bodies affect one another across empty space, so that in reality force is exerted from a distance. Physics believes it is justified in assuming that a material body does not affect our senses of touch and warmth by direct contact, because there must be a certain distance, even if very small, between the body and the place where it touches the skin. From this he concludes further that what we sense as the hardness or warmth of a body, for example, is only the reaction of the peripheral nerves of our senses of touch and warmth to the *molecular forces* of bodies which act upon them across empty space.

These considerations of the physicist are amplified by those of the psycho-physicist in the form of a science of specific sense-energies. J. Müller* has shown that each sense can be affected only in a characteristic manner which is conditioned by its structure, so that it always reacts in the same way to any external stimulus. If the optic nerve is stimulated, there is a sensation of light, whether the stimulus is in the form of pressure, electric current, or light. On the other hand, the same external phenomenon produces quite different sensations, according to which sense organ transmits it. This leads to the conclusion that there is only *one* kind of phenomenon in the external world, namely motion, and that the many aspects of the world which we perceive derive essentially from the reaction of our senses to this phenomenon. According to this view, we do not perceive the external world. itself, but merely the subjective sensations which it releases in us.

Thus physiology is added to physics. Physics deals with the phenomena occurring outside our organism to which our perceptions correspond; physiology aims to investigate the processes that occur in man's body when he experiences a certain sense impression. It shows that the epidermis is completely insensitive to external stimuli. In order to reach the nerves connected with our sense of touch on the periphery of the body, an external vibration must first be transmitted through the epidermis. In the case of hearing and vision the external motion is further modified through a number of organs in these sense-tools, before it reaches the corresponding nerve. These effects, produced in the organs at the periphery of the body, now have to be conducted through the nerve to the central organ, where sensations are finally produced through purely mechanical processes in the brain. It is obvious that the stimulus which acts on the sense organ is so changed through these modifications that there can be no similarity between what first affected the sense organs, and the sensations that finally arise in consciousness. The result of these considerations is summed up by Hartmann in the following words: "The content of consciousness consists fundamentally of the sensations that are the soul's reflex response to processes of movement in the uppermost part of the brain, and these have not the slightest resemblance to the molecular movements that called them into being."[22] If this line of thought is correct and is pursued to its conclusion, it must then be admitted that our consciousness does not contain the slightest element of what could be called external existence. To the physical and physiological arguments against so-called "naive realism" Hartmann adds further objections which he describes as essentially philosophical. A logical examination of the first two objections reveals that in fact one can arrive at the above result only by first assuming the existence and interrelations of external things, as ordinary naive consciousness does, and then

---

[22] *Grundproblem (Fundamental Problem)*, p. 37.

investigating how this external world enters our consciousness by means of our organism. We have seen that between receiving a sense impression and becoming conscious of a sensation, every trace of such an external world is lost, and all that remains in consciousness are our representations. We must therefore assume that our picture of the external world is built up by the soul, using the material of sensations. First of all, a spatial picture is constructed using the sensations produced by sight and touch, and sensations arising from the other senses are then added. When we are compelled to think of a certain complex of sensations as connected, we are led to the concept of substance, which we consider to be the carrier of sensations. If we notice that some sensations associated with a substance disappear, while others arise, we ascribe this to a change regulated by the causal laws in the world of phenomena. According to this view, our whole world-picture is composed of subjective sensations arranged by our own soul-activity. Hartmann says: "Thus all that the subject perceives are modifications of its own soul-condition and nothing else."[23]

Let us examine how this conviction is arrived at. The argument may be summarized as follows: If an external world exists then we do not perceive it as such, but through our organism transform it into a world of representations. When followed out consistently, this is a self-canceling assumption. In any case, can this argument be used to establish any conviction at all? Are we justified in regarding our given world-picture as a subjective content of representations, just because we arrive inevitably at this conclusion if we start from the assumption made by naive consciousness? After all, the aim was just to prove this assumption invalid. It should then be possible for an assertion to be wrong, and yet lead to a

---

[23] *Philosophische Monatshefte*, XXVI, p., XXVI, p. 390, Heidelberg, 1890.

correct result. This can indeed happen somewhere, but the result cannot then be said to have been *proved* by the assertion.

The view which accepts the reality of our directly given picture of the world as certain and beyond doubt, is usually called naive realism. The opposite view, which regards this world-picture as merely the content of our consciousness, is called transcendental idealism. Thus the preceding discussion could also be summarized as follows: *Transcendental idealism demonstrates its truth by using the same premises as the naive realism which it aims to refute.* Transcendental idealism is justified if naive realism is proved incorrect, but its incorrectness is only demonstrated by means of the incorrect view itself. Once this is realized there is no alternative but to abandon this path and to attempt to arrive at another view of the world. Does this mean proceeding by trial and error until we happen to hit on the right one? That is Hartmann's approach when he believes his epistemological standpoint established on the grounds that his view explains the phenomena, whereas others do not. According to him the various worldviews are engaged in a sort of struggle for existence, in which the fittest is ultimately accepted as victor. But the inconsistency of this procedure is immediately apparent, for there might well be other hypotheses which would explain the phenomena *equally* satisfactorily. For this reason we prefer to adhere to the above argument for the refuting of naive realism, and investigate precisely where its weakness lies. After all, naive realism is the viewpoint from which we all start. It is therefore the proper starting-point for a critical investigation. By recognizing its shortcomings we shall be led to the right path much more surely than by simply trusting to luck. The subjectivism outlined above is based on *the use of thinking* for elaborating certain facts. This presupposes that, starting from certain facts, a correct conclusion can be attained through logical thinking (logical combination of particular observations). But the *justification* for using thinking in this way is not examined by this philosophical approach. This is its weakness. While naïve realism begins by assuming that the content of perceptual experience as objective reality without examining if this is so, the standpoint just characterized sets out from the equally uncritical conviction that thinking can be used to arrive at scientifically valid conclusions. In contrast to naïve realism, this view could be called naïve rationalism. To justify this term, a brief comment on the concept of "naive" is necessary here. A. Döring tries to define this concept in his essay, *Über den Begriff des naiven Realismus (Concerning the Concept of naive Realism)*. He says: "The concept 'naive' designates the zero point in the scale of reflection about one's own relation to what one is doing. A naive content may well be correct, for although it is unreflecting and therefore simply non-critical or uncritical, this lack of reflection and criticism excludes the objective assurance of truth, and includes the possibility and danger of error, yet by no means necessitates them. One can be equally naive in one's life of feeling and will, as in the life of representing and thinking in the widest sense; furthermore, one may express this inner life in a naive manner rather than repressing and modifying it through consideration and reflection. To be naive means not to be influenced, or at least not consciously influenced by tradition, education or rules; it means to be, in all spheres of life, what the root of the word: 'nativus' implies. i.e., unconscious, impulsive, instinctive, daimonic." Starting from this, we will endeavor to define "naive" still more precisely. In all our activities, two things must be taken into account: the activity itself, and our knowledge of its lawfulness. We may be completely absorbed in the activity without worrying about its lawfulness. The artist is in this position when he does not reflect about the laws according to which he creates, but *applies* them, using feeling and sensitivity. We may call him "naive." It is possible, however, to observe oneself, and enquire into the laws inherent in one's own activity, thus abandoning the naive consciousness just described through knowing exactly the scope of and justification for what one does. This I shall call *critical*. I believe this definition comes nearest to the meaning of this concept as it has been used in philosophy, with greater or lesser clarity, ever since Kant. Critical reflection then is the opposite of the naive approach. A critical attitude is one that comes to grips with the laws of its own activity in order to discover their reliability and limits. Epistemology can only be a critical science. Its object is an eminently subjective activity of man: *cognition*, and it seeks to demonstrate *the laws inherent in cognition*. Thus all naïveté must be excluded from this science. Its strengths lie in doing precisely what many thinkers, inclined more toward practical action, pride themselves that they never done: namely, "thinking about thinking."

IV.

THE STARTING POINT OF EPISTEMOLOGY

As we have seen in the preceding chapters, an epistemological investigation must begin by rejecting existing knowledge. Knowledge is something brought into existence by the human being – something that has arisen through human activity. If a theory of knowledge is really to explain the whole sphere of knowledge then it must start from something still quite untouched by the activity of thinking, and moreover, something that lends to this activity its first impulse. This starting point must lie outside the act of cognition, it must not itself be knowledge. But it must be sought immediately prior to cognition, so that the very next step the knower takes beyond it is the act of cognition. This absolute starting point must be determined in such a way that admits nothing already derived from the act of knowing.

Only our immediately given world-image (*Weltbild*) can offer such a starting point, that is, that which lies before us prior to subjecting it to the process of cognition in any way, before we have asserted or decided anything about it by means of thinking. This "directly given" is what passes us by, and what we pass by, disconnected but still not divided into individual entities,[24] in which nothing appears distinguished from, related to, or determined by anything else. At this stage, so to speak, no object or event is yet more important or significant than any other. The most rudimentary organ of an animal, which, in the light of further knowledge may turn out to be quite unimportant for its development and life, appears before us with the same claims for our attention as the noblest and most essential part of the organism. Before our conceptual activity

---

[24] The isolation of individual details out of the whole undifferentiated image of the world is already a deed of thinking activity.

begins, the world-picture contains neither substance, quality, nor cause and effect; distinction between matter and spirit, body and soul, do not yet exist. Furthermore any other predicates must be excluded at this stage. The picture can be considered neither as reality nor as appearance, neither subjective nor objective, neither as chance nor as necessity; whether it is a "thing-in-itself" or mere representation cannot be decided at this stage. As we have seen, a knowledge of physics or physiology which leads to a classification of the "given" under one or the other of the above headings cannot be the basis for a theory of knowledge.

If a being with a fully developed human intelligence were suddenly created out of nothing and then confronted with the world, the first impression on his senses and his thinking would be something like what I have just characterized as the unmediated given. In practice, we never encountered the given in this form – that is, there is never an experienced division between a pure, passive turning toward the given and the cognitive grasp of the given. This fact could lead to doubt about my description of the starting point for a theory of knowledge. Hartmann says for example: "We are not concerned with the hypothetical content of consciousness in a child which is just becoming conscious or in an animal at the lowest level of life, since the philosophizing human being has no experience of this; if he tries to reconstruct the content of consciousness of beings on primitive biogenetic or ontogenetic levels, he must base his conclusions on the way he experiences his own consciousness. Our first task, therefore, is to establish the content of man's consciousness when he begins philosophical reflection."[25] The objection to this, however, is that the world-picture with which we begin philosophical reflection already contains predicates mediated through cognition. These cannot be accepted uncritically, but must be carefully removed from the world-

---

[25] *Grundproblem (The Fundamental Problem)*, p. 1.

picture so that it can be considered free of anything introduced through the process of knowledge. The division between the "given" and they "known" will not in fact coincide with any stage of human development; the boundary must be drawn artificially. But this can be done at every level of development so long as we draw the dividing line correctly between what confronts us free of all cognitive determinations, and what cognition subsequently makes of it.

It might be objected here that I have already made use of a number of conceptual definitions in order to extract from the world-picture as it appears when completed by man, that other world-picture which I described as the directly given. But against this the following can be said: A number of conceptual definitions, what we have extracted by means of thought does not characterized the directly given, nor define or express anything about it; what it does is to guide our attention to the dividing line where the starting point of cognition is to be discovered. The question of truth or error, correctness or incorrectness, does not enter into this statement, which is concerned with the moment preceding the point where a theory of knowledge begins. It serves merely to guide us deliberately to this starting point. No one proceeding to consider epistemological questions could possibly be said to be standing at the starting point of cognition, for he already possesses a certain amount of knowledge. To remove all that has been contributed by cognition, and to establish a precognitive starting point, can only be done conceptually. But such concepts are not of value as knowledge; they have the purely negative function of removing from sight all that belongs to knowledge of leading us to the point where knowledge begins. These considerations act as signposts pointing to where cognition first appears, but at this stage do not themselves form part of the act of cognition. Whatever the epistemologist proposes in order to establish his starting point raises, to begin with, no question of truth or error, but only of its suitability for this task. All error is also excluded from this starting point, for error can begin only with cognition, and therefore cannot arise before cognition sets in.

Only a theory of knowledge that starts from considerations of this kind can claim to observe this last principle. If the starting point is some object (or subject) to which a conceptual determination is attached, then the possibility of error is already present in the starting point, namely the determination of itself. Justification of the determination will depend upon the laws inherent in the act of cognition, but these laws can be discovered only in the course of the investigation. Error is only excluded when one says: I remove from my world-picture all determinations arrived at through cognition and retain only what enters the horizon of my activity without activity on my part. When on principle I make no claim I also make no mistake.

Error, in relation to knowledge, can occur only within the act of cognition. Sense deceptions are not errors. That the moon upon rising appears larger than it does at its zenith is not an error but a fact governed by the laws of nature. A mistake in knowledge would occur only if, in using thinking combine the given perceptions, we interpret this "larger" and "smaller" in an incorrect manner. This interpretation, however, lies within the act of cognition.

To understand cognition exactly in its full being, its origin and starting point must doubtless first be grasped. It is clear, furthermore, that what precedes this primary starting point must not be included in an explanation of cognition, but must be presupposed. Investigation of the essence of what is here presupposed, is the task of the various branches of scientific knowledge. The present aim, however, is not to acquire specific knowledge of this or that element, but to investigate cognition itself. Until we have understood the act of knowledge, we cannot judge the significance of statements about the content of the world arrived at through the act of cognition.

This is why the directly given is not determined as long as the relation of such a determination to what is to be determined is not known. Even the concept: "directly given" includes no statement about what precedes cognition. Its only purpose is to point to this given, to turn our attention to it. At the starting point of a theory of knowledge, conceptual form is only the first initial relation between cognition and the content of the world. This description even allows for the possibility that the total content of the world would turn out to be only a figment of our own "I," which would mean that exclusive subjectivism would be true; subjectivism is not something that exists as given. It can only be a conclusion drawn from considerations based on cognition, i.e. it would have to be confirmed by the theory of knowledge; it could not be assumed as its basis.

This directly given content includes everything that enters our experience in the widest sense: sensations, perceptions, opinions, feelings, deeds, pictures of dreams and imaginations, representations, concepts and ideas.

Illusions and hallucinations too, at this stage are equal to the rest of the given, for their relation to other perceptions can review be revealed only through observation based on cognition.

When epistemology starts from the assumption that all the elements just mentioned constitute the content of our consciousness, the following question immediately arises: How is it possible for us to go beyond our consciousness and recognize actual existence; where can the leap be made from subjectivity to the transsubjective? When such an assumption is not made, the situation is different. Both consciousness and the representation of the "I" are, to begin with only parts of the directly given and the relationship of the latter to the two former must be discovered by means of cognition. Cognition is not to be defined in terms of consciousness, but vice versa: both consciousness and the relation between the subject and object in terms of cognition. Since the "given" is originally without predicates, the question becomes how can it be determined at all: how can any start be made with cognition? How does one part of the world-picture come to be designated as perception and the other as concept, one thing as existence, another as appearance, this as cause and that as effect; how is it that we can separate ourselves from what is objective and regard ourselves as "I" in contrast to the "not-I?"

We must find the bridge from the world as given to the world-picture that we build up through cognition. Here however, we meet with the following difficulty: As long as we merely stare passively at the given will never find a point of attack where we can gain a foothold, and from where we can proceed with cognition. Somewhere in the given we must find a place where we can set to work, where something exists which is akin to cognition; if everything were really only given, we could do no more than merely stare into the external world and stare indifferently into the inner world of our individuality. We would at most be able to describe things as something external to us; we should never be able to understand them. Our concepts would have a purely external relation to that to which they referred; they would not be inwardly related to it. For real cognition depends on finding a sphere somewhere in the given where our cognizing activity is not merely presuppose something given, but finds itself active in the very essence of the given. In other words, precisely through strict adherence to the given as merely given it must become apparent that not everything in the given fits this description. Insistence on the given alone must lead to the discovery of something which goes beyond the given. The reason for so insisting is not to establish some arbitrary starting point for a theory of knowledge, but to discover the true one. In this sense, the given also includes what according to its very nature is not-given. The latter would appear, to begin with, as merely formally a part of the given, but on closer scrutiny, would reveal its true nature of its own accord.

The whole difficulty in understanding cognition comes in the fact that we ourselves do not create the content of the world. If we did this, cognition would not exist at all. I can only ask questions about something which is "given" to me. Something that I create myself I also determine myself, so that I need not ask for an explanation of it.

This is the second step in our theory of knowledge. It consists in the postulate: In the sphere of the given there must be something in relation to which our activity does not hover in emptiness, but where the content of the world itself enters this activity.

Just as we specified that the starting point of a theory of knowledge must precede all cognition so the preconceptions could not cloud our cognitive activity, so now we specify the next step so that there can be no question of error or incorrect judgment. For this step prejudges nothing, but simply specifies what conditions must obtain if knowledge is to arise at all. It is essential that through critical reflection we become fully conscious of the fact that is we who postulate what characteristic feature must be possessed by that part of the world-content with which our cognitive activity can make a start.

This, in fact, is the only thing we can do. The world-content as given is completely undetermined. No part of it of its own accord can provide the occasion for setting it up as a starting point to bring order out of chaos. The activity of thinking must therefore issue a decree and declare what characteristics such part must manifest. Such a decree in no way infringes upon the qualities of the given. It does not introduce any arbitrary assumptions into epistemology. In fact, it asserts nothing about the given at all, but states only that if knowledge is to be explained, then we must look for some point in the given that has the characteristics described above. If such a region can be found, cognition can be explained, but not otherwise. Thus, while the "given" provides a general starting point for our account, our focus must now be narrowed to this particular point.

Let us now take a closer look at this demand. Where, within the given, do we find something that is not merely given, but only given insofar as it is brought forth in the actual act of cognition?

It is essential to realize that this bringing-forth must also be immediately given. Deduction must not be necessary in order to recognize it. This at once indicates the sense that impressions do not meet our requirements, for we cannot know directly but only indirectly that sense impressions do not occur without activity in our on our part; this we discover only by considering physical and physiological factors. But we know quite immediately that concepts and ideas arise only through cognitive activity and through this enter the sphere of the directly given. In this respect concepts and ideas do not deceive anyone. A hallucination may appear as something externally given but we would never take our concepts to be something given without our thinking activity. A lunatic regards things and relations as real to which are applied the predicate "reality," although in fact they are not real; but he would never say that his concepts and ideas entered the sphere of the given without his own activity. It is a characteristic feature of the rest of the world-content that it must be given if we are to experience it; the only case in which the opposite occurs is that of concepts and ideas: these we must bring forth if we are to experience them. Concepts and ideas alone are given to us in a form that is called intellectual intuition (*intellektuelle Anschauung*). Kant and the later philosophers who follow in his steps completely deny this ability to humans, because it is said that all thinking refers only to objects and does not itself produce anything. In intellectual intuition content must be contained within the thought-form itself. But is this not precisely the case with pure concepts and ideas?

(By concept I mean a principle by which the unconnected elements of perception are bound into a unity. Causality, for example, is a concept. An idea is a concept with a greater content. Organism, considered quite abstractly, is an idea.) One need only look at them [concepts and ideas] in the form which they possess while they are still free of all empirical content. If one wants to grasp the pure concept of causality, then one must not hold to a particular instance, nor even to the sum of instances, but only the concept itself. Causes and effects we must seek in the world, but we must produce *causality* as a thought-form before we can look for the relation in the world. If one wanted to cling to the Kantian dictum that concepts without perceptions are empty, one could not think of determining the "given" world through concepts. Let us imagine that two elements of the world, *a* and *b* are given. If I am to seek a relation between them I must do so with the help of the principle of definite content. I can only produce this through the act of cognition – I cannot take it from the objects as given, for their relation is to be determined with the aid of the same principle. Such a principle, by which we determine reality, belongs only to a purely conceptual sphere.

Before proceeding further, a possible objection must be considered. It might appear that this discussion is unconsciously introducing the representation of the "I," of the "personal subject," and using it without first justifying it. For example, in statements like "we produce concepts" or "we insist on this or that." But, in fact, my explanation contains nothing which implies that such statements are more than turns of phrase. As shown earlier, the fact that the act of cognition depends upon and proceeds from an "I," can be established only through considerations which themselves make use of cognition. Thus, to begin with, the discussion must be limited to the act of cognition alone, without considering the cognizing subject. All that has been established thus far is the fact that something "given" exists; and that somewhere in this "given" the above described postulate arises; and lastly, that this postulate corresponds to the sphere of concepts and ideas. This is not to deny that its source is the "I." But these two initial steps in the theory of knowledge must first be defined in their pure form.

V.

COGNITION AND REALITY

Concepts and ideas comprise part of the given, but at the same time lead beyond it. This makes it possible to determine the nature of the remaining activity of cognition. Through a postulate we have separated a particular part from the rest of the given content; this was done because it lies in the nature of cognition to start with just this part. Thus it was separated only to allow us to understand the act of cognition. In so doing we must be clear that we have artificially torn apart the unity of the world-content. We must realize that what we have separated has a necessary connection to that content irrespective of our postulate. This provides the next step in the theory of knowledge; it must consist of restoring that unity which we tore apart in order to make knowledge possible. This restoration takes place in *thinking* of the world as given. Our thinking contemplation of the world brings about the actual union of the two parts of the world-content: the part we survey as given on the horizon of our experience, and the part that has to be produced in the act of cognition before it can be given. The act of cognition is the synthesis of these two elements. Indeed, in every single act of cognition, one part appears as something produced in this act itself, and it is brought by the same act to the merely given. This part, in actual fact, is always so produced, and only appears as something given at the beginning of epistemology.

To permeate the given world with concepts and ideas is a *thinking* contemplation of things. Thus thinking is actually the act through which knowledge is mediated. Only when thinking, out of itself, orders the content of the world picture, can knowledge come about. Thinking itself is an activity that brings forth a content of its own in the moment of knowing. Insofar as the content that is cognized issues from thinking, it contains no problems for cognition. We have only to observe it: the very nature of what we observe is given to us directly. A *description* of thinking is also at the same time the science of thinking. Logic too has always been a description of thought forms, never a science that demonstrates anything. Demonstrative evidence is only called for when the content of thought is synthesized with some other content of the world. Gideon Spicker is therefore quite right when he says in his book, *Lessings Weltanschauung (Lessing's Worldview)*, page 5, "We can never experience, either empirically or logically, whether thinking in itself is correct." One could add to this that with thinking, all demonstration [that is, providing evidence] ceases, for demonstration presupposes thinking. One may be able to demonstrate a particular fact, but no one is able to demonstrate the validity of demonstration. We can only describe what demonstration is. In logic all theory is empiricism – in this science there is only observation. But when we want to know something other than thinking, we can do so only with the help of thinking – that is, thinking has to approach something given and transform the chaotic relationship with the world picture into a systematic one. Thinking therefore approaches the given content as an organizing principle. The process takes place as follows: Thinking first lifts out certain entities from the totality of the world-whole. In the given there is actually no singularity, for all is continuously blended. Then thinking relates these separate entities to each other in accordance with the thought-forms it produces, and lastly determines the outcome of this relationship. When thinking restores a relationship between two separate sections of the world-content, it does not do so arbitrarily. Thinking waits for what comes to light of its own accord as result of restoring the relationship. By establishing relation between two distinct parts of the world content, thinking of itself has determined absolutely nothing about them. Thinking waits for what comes to light of its own accord as a result of restoring the relationship. It is this result alone that is knowledge of that particular section of the world content. If this particular section of the world content were unable to express anything about itself through that relationship, then this attempt made by thinking would fail, and one would have to try again. All knowledge depends on establishing a correct relationship between two or more elements of reality and grasping the result of this.

There is no doubt that many of our attempts to grasp things by means of thinking fail; this is apparent not only in the history of science, but also in ordinary life; it is just that in the simple cases we usually encounter, the right concept replaces the wrong one so quickly that the latter does not come to consciousness at all or does so only seldom.

When Kant speaks of the "the synthetic unity of apperception" is evident that he had some inkling of what we have shown here to be the activity of thinking, the purpose of which is to organize the world-content systematically. But that he thought to derive *a priori* laws of pure science from the rules according to which this synthesis takes place shows how little this inkling brought to his consciousness the essential task of thinking. He did not realize that this synthetic activity of thinking is only a *preparation* for discovering actual natural laws. Suppose, for example, that we detach a content, *a*, and another content, *b*, from the given. If we are to gain knowledge of the law connecting *a* and *b*, then thinking was first relate *a* and *b* so that through this relationship the connection between them presents itself as given. The actual content of a law of nature is derived from the given, and the task of thinking is merely to provide an occasion for the natural law to become evident by placing the elements of the given in that relationship. No objective laws follow from the synthetic activity of thinking alone.

We must now ask what part thinking plays in building up our scientific world-picture, in contrast to the merely given world-picture. Our discussion shows that thinking provides the form of lawfulness. In the example given above, let us assume *a* to be the cause and *b* the effect. The fact that *a* and *b* are causally connected could never become knowledge if thinking were not able to form the concept of causality. Yet in order to recognize, in a given case, that *a* is the cause and *b* the effect, it is necessary for *a* and *b* to correspond to what we understand by cause and effect. And this is true of all other categories of thinking as well.

At this point it will be useful to refer briefly to Hume's* description of the concept of causality. Hume said that our concepts of cause and effect are due solely to *habit*. We so often notice that a particular event is followed by another that accordingly we form the habit of thinking of them as causally connected, i.e. we expect the second event to occur whenever we observe the first. But this viewpoint stems from a mistaken representation of the relationship concerned in causality. Suppose that I always meet the same people every day for a number of days when I leave my house; it is true that I shall then gradually come to expect the two events to follow one another, but in this case it would never occur to me to look for a causal connection between the other persons and my own appearance at the same spot. I would look to quite different elements of the world-content in order to explain the facts involved. In fact, we never do determine a causal connection to be such from its sequence in time, but from its own content as part of the world-content which is that of cause and effect.

The activity of thinking is only a formal one in bringing about our scientific world-picture, and it follows that no cognition can have content which is *a priori* – which is established prior to observation (and therefore divorced from the given). Content must rather be derived wholly from observation. In this sense all our knowledge is empirical. Nor is it possible to see how it could be otherwise. Kant's judgments *a priori* are not cognition, but only postulates. In the Kantian sense one can always say: If a thing is to be the object of any kind of experience, then it must conform

152

to certain laws. Laws in this sense are prescriptions that the subject prescribes for the objects. Yet one would expect that if we are to attain knowledge of the given it must be derived, not from the subject, but from the object.

Thinking says nothing *a priori* about the given; it produces the thought-forms on the basis of which the conformity to law of the phenomena becomes apparent *a posteriori*.

Seen in this light, it is obvious that one can say nothing a priori about the degree of certainty of a judgment attained through cognition. For certainty, too, can be derived only from the given. To this it could be objected that observation only shows that some connection between phenomena once occurred, but *not* that such a connection must occur, and in similar cases always will occur. This assumption is also wrong. When I recognize some particular connection between elements of the world-picture, this connection is provided by these elements themselves; it is not something I think into them, but is an essential part of them, and must necessarily be present whenever the elements themselves are present.

Only if it is considered that scientific effort is merely a matter of combining facts of experience according to subjective principles which are quite external to the facts themselves, — only such an outlook could believe that *a* and *b* may be connected by one law today and by another tomorrow (John Stuart Mill).* Someone who recognizes that the laws of nature originate in the given and therefore themselves constitute the connection between the phenomena and determine them, will not describe laws discovered by observation as merely of comparative universality. This is not to assert that a natural law which at one stage we assume to be correct must therefore be universally valid as well. When a later event disproves a law, this does not imply that the law had only a limited validity when first discovered, but rather that we failed to ascertain it with complete accuracy. A true law of nature is simply the expression of

153

a connection within the given world-picture, and it exists as little without the facts it governs as the facts exist without the law.

We have established that the nature of the activity of cognition is to permeate the given world-picture with concepts and ideas by means of thinking. What follows from this fact? If the directly-given were a totality, complete in itself, then such an elaboration of it by means of cognition would be both impossible and unnecessary. We should then simply accept the given as it is, and would be satisfied with it in that form. The act of cognition is possible only because something is hidden in the given which *does not* appear in its immediate aspect, but reveals itself only through the order that thinking brings to the given. What lies within the given *before* it has been elaborated by thought is not its full totality.

This becomes clearer when we consider more closely the factors pertinent to the act of cognition. The first of these is the given. That it is given is not a feature of the given, but an expression denoting its relation to the second factor in cognition. Thus what this given may be is completely undecided by this designation. In the act of cognition thinking finds the second factor: the conceptual content of the given, to be necessarily united with the given. We must ask ourselves:

(1) Where does the separation between given and concepts lie?

2) Where are they united?

Both these questions have been answered in the preceding investigation. The separation exists solely in the act of cognition, the union lies in the given. It follows from this that the conceptual content is only part of the given, and that the act of cognition consists in uniting the parts of the world picture that are given it to it separately. Therefore, the given world-picture becomes complete only through that other, indirect kind of given which is brought to it by thinking. The immediate aspect of the world-picture reveals itself as quite incomplete to begin with.

If, in the world-content, the thought-content were united with the given from the first, no knowledge would exist, and the need to go beyond the given would never arise. If, on the other hand, we were to produce the whole content of the world in and by means of thinking alone, no knowledge would exist either. What we ourselves produce we have no need to know. Knowledge rests on the fact that the world-content is originally given to us in an incomplete form; it possesses an essential aspect beyond what is immediately offered. The second aspect of the world-content, which is not originally given, is revealed through thinking. That which appears to us something separate in thinking, is therefore not empty form, but comprises the sum of those determinations (categories) that are the form of the rest of the world content. The world-content can be called reality only in the form it attains when the two aspects described above have been united through knowledge.

VI.
THEORY OF KNOWLEDGE FREE
OF ASSUMPTIONS, AND FICHTE'S
SCIENCE OF KNOWLEDGE

We have now identified the idea of knowledge. This idea is immediately given to human consciousness insofar as it cognizes. Both outer and inner percepts, as well as its own presence are immediately given to the "I," which is the center of consciousness. (It is hardly necessary to they say that here "center" is not meant to denote any particular theory of consciousness, but is used merely for the sake of brevity in order to denote the collective physiognomy of consciousness.) The "I" feels a need to discover more in the given than is immediately contained in it. In contrast to the given world, a second world – the world of thinking – rises up to meet the "I" and the "I" unites the two through its own free decision, realizing what we identified as the idea of knowledge. Here we see the fundamental difference between the way the concept and the directly given are united within to object of human consciousness to form full reality, and the way they are found united in the remainder of the world-content. In the rest of the world-picture we must conceive of an original union that is an inherent necessity; an artificial separation occurs only in relation to knowledge at the point where cognition begins; cognition then cancels out this separation once more, in accordance with the original nature of the objective world. But in human consciousness the situation is different. Here the union of the two factors of reality depends on the activity of consciousness. In all other objects the separation has no significance for the objects themselves, but only for knowledge. Their union is original and their separation is derived. Cognition separates them only because its nature is such that it cannot grasp their union without having first separated them. But the separation of concept and the given

156

reality of consciousness [cognition] is original, and their union is derived; which is why cognition has the nature described here. Just because, for consciousness, idea and given are necessarily separated, for consciousness the whole of reality divides into these two factors; and again, just because consciousness can effect their union only by its own activity, it can arrive at full reality only by performing the act of cognition. All other categories (ideas), prior to being taken up by cognition, are necessarily united with their corresponding forms of the given. But the idea of knowing can be united with its corresponding given only by the activity of consciousness. Actual consciousness exists only if it actualizes itself. I believe that I've now cleared the ground sufficiently to enable us to understand Fichte's *Science of Knowledge* through recognition of the fundamental mistake contained in it. Of all Kant's successors, Fichte is the one who felt most keenly that only a theory of consciousness could provide the foundation for knowledge in any form, yet he never came to recognize why this is so. He felt that what I've called the second step in theory of knowledge, and which I formulated as a postulate, must be actively performed by the "I." This can be seen, for example, from these words: "The science of knowledge thus arises, to the extent that it should be a systematic science, just like all possible sciences insofar as they are to be systematic, is built up through a determination of freedom; which freedom, in the science of knowledge, is particularly determined: to become conscious of the general manner of acting of the intelligence ... By means of this free act, something which is in itself already form, namely, the necessary act of the intelligence, is taken up as content and put into a new form, that is, the form of knowledge or of consciousness ..." What does Fichte mean by the "acting of intelligence" if we express in clear concepts what he dimly felt? Nothing other than the realization of the idea of cognition in consciousness. Had Fichte been clear about this he would have formulated the above principle as follows: A science of knowledge has the task of bringing to consciousness the act of cognition, in so far as it is still

157

an unconscious activity of the "I": it must show that to objectify the idea of cognition is a necessary deed of the "I." In his attempt to define the activity of the "I," Fichte comes to the conclusion: "The 'I' as absolute subject is something, the being (essence) of which consists merely in positing its own existence."[26] For Fichte, this positing of the "I" is the primal unconditioned deed, which "is the basis of all consciousness."[27] Therefore, in Fichte's sense too, the "I" can begin to be active only through an absolute original decision. But for Fichte it is impossible to find the actual content of the original activity posited by the "I." He had nothing toward which this activity could be directed or by which it could be determined. The "I" is to do something, but what is it to do? Fichte did not formulate the concept of knowledge that the "I" is to realize, and in consequence he strove in vain to identify any further activity of the "I" beyond the original deed. In fact, he finally stated that to investigate any such further activity does not lie within the scope of theory. In his deduction of representation, he does not begin from any absolute activity of the "I" or of the "not-I," but he starts from a state of determination which, at the same time, itself determines, because in his view nothing else is, or can be contained directly in consciousness. What in turn determines the state of determination is left completely undecided in his theory; and because of this uncertainty, one is forced beyond theory into practical application of the science of knowledge.[28] However, through this statement Fichte completely abolishes all cognition. For the practical activity of the "I" belongs to a different sphere altogether. The positing which I put forward above can clearly be produced by the "I" only in an

---

[26] *Über den Begriff der Wissenschaftslehre oder der sogennanten Philosophie (On The Concept of the Science of Knowledge or So-Called Philosophy), Sämtliche Werke (Complete Works) I*, Berlin 1845, p. 71 f.
[27] *Grundlage der gesamten Wissenschaftslehre, Sämtliche Werke (Complete Works) I*, p. 97.
[28] *Sämtliche Werke (Complete Works) I*, p. 91.

act which is free, which is not first determined; but when the "I" cognizes, the important point is that the decision to do so is directed toward producing the idea of cognition. No doubt the "I" can do much else through free decision. But if epistemology is to be the foundation of all knowledge, the decisive point is not to have a definition of an "I" that is "free," but of an "I" that "cognizes." Fichte has allowed himself to be too much influenced by his subjective inclinations to present the freedom of the human personality in the clearest possible light. Harms, in his address, *On the Philosophy of Fichte*, (p. 15) rightly says: "His worldview is predominantly and exclusively ethical, and his theory of knowledge has no other feature." Cognition would have no task to fulfill whatever if all spheres of reality were given in their totality. But the "I," so long as it has not been inserted by thinking into the systematic whole of the world-picture, also exists as something merely directly given, so that it does not suffice to point to its activity. Yet Fichte is of the opinion that where the "I" is concerned, all that is necessary is to seek and find it. "We have to search for the absolute, first, and unconditioned fundamental principle of human knowledge. It cannot be proven nor determined if it is to be absolute first principle."[29] We have seen that the only instance where proof and definitions are not required is in regard to the content of pure logic.[30] The "I," however, belongs to reality, where it is necessary to establish the presence of this or that category within the given. This Fichte does not do. And this is why he gave his science of knowledge a mistaken form. Zeller[31] remarks that the logical formulas by which Fichte attempts to arrive at the concept of the "I" only lightly hide his predetermined purpose to reach his goal at any cost, so that the "I" could become his starting point. These words refer to the first form in which Fichte

---

[29] *Sämtliche Werke (Complete Works) I*, p. 178.
[30] *Sämtliche Werke (Complete Works) I*, p. 91.
[31] *Geschichte der deutschen Philosophie seit Leibniz (History of German Philosophy since Leibniz)*, Munich 1871 to 1875, p. 606.

presented his science of knowledge in 1794. When it is realized that, owing to the whole trend of his philosophy, Fichte could not be content with any starting point for knowledge other than an absolute decree, it becomes clear that he has only two possibilities for making this beginning appear intelligible. One possibility is to focus the attention on one or another of the empirical activities of consciousness, and then crystallize out the pure concept of the "I" by gradually stripping away everything that did not originally belong to consciousness. The other possibility is to start directly with the original activity of the "I," and then to bring its nature to light through self-contemplation and self-observation. Fichte chose the first possibility at the beginning of his philosophical path, but gradually went over to the second.

On the basis of Kant's synthesis of "transcendental apperception" Fichte came to the conclusion that the activity of the "I" consists entirely in combining the material of experience into the form of judgment. To judge means to combine predicate with subject. This is stated purely formally in the expression: $a = a$. This proposition could not be made if the unknown factor x which unites the two a's did not rest on an absolute ability of the "I", to posit. For the proposition does not mean a exists, but rather: if a exists, then so does a. In other words there is no question of positing a absolutely. In order, therefore, to arrive at something which is valid absolutely and unconditionally the only possibility is to declare the act of positing as such to be absolute. Therefore, while a is conditional the positing of a is itself unconditional. This positing, however, is a deed of the "I." To the "I" is ascribed the absolute and unconditional ability to posit. In the proposition $a = a$, one a is posited only because the other a is already posited, and indeed is posited by the I. "If a is posited in the I, then it is posited."[32] This connection is possible only on condition that

---

[32] *Sämtliche Werke (Complete Works) I*, p. 94.

there exists in the I something which is always constant, something that leads over from one *a* to the other. The above mentioned *x* is based on this constant element. The "I" which posits the one *a* is the same as the "I" which posits the other *a*. This means that I = I. This proposition expressed in the form of a judgment: If the "I" exists, then the "I" exists, is meaningless. The "I" is not posited by presupposing another "I"; it presupposes itself. This means: the "I" simply is, absolutely and unconditionally. The hypothetical form of a judgment, which is the form of all judgments, when an absolute "I" is not presupposed, here is transformed into a principle of absolute existence: "I" simply am. Fichte also expresses this as follows: "The 'I' originally and absolutely posits its own being."[33] This whole deduction of Fichte's is clearly nothing but a kind of pedagogical discussion, the aim of which is to guide his reader to the point where knowledge of the unconditional activity of the "I" dawns in him. His aim is to bring the activity of the "I" emphatically home to the reader, for without this activity there is no "I."

Let us now survey Fichte's line of thought once more. On closer inspection one sees that there is a break in its sequence; a break, indeed, of a kind that casts doubt upon the correctness of his view of the original deed [*Tathandlung*] of the "I." What is essentially absolute when the "I" posits? The judgment is made: If *a* exists, then *a* is. The *a* is posited by the "I." There can, therefore, be no doubt about the positing as such. Even if the "I" is free in so far as its own activity is concerned, nevertheless the "I" cannot but posit something. It cannot posit "activity, as such, by itself," but only a definite activity. In short: the positing must have a content. However, the "I" cannot derive this content from itself, for by itself it can do no more than eternally posit its own positing. Therefore there must be something which is produced by this positing, by this absolute activity of the "I." Unless the "I" sets to work on something given

---

[33] *Sämtliche Werke (Complete Works) I*, p. 98.

which it posits, it can do "nothing," and therefore cannot posit either. Fichte's own principle actually shows this: the "I" posits its existence, Existence is a category. This means we have arrived at our principle: the activity of the "I" is to posit, by a free decision, the concepts and ideas of the given. Fichte arrives at this conclusion only because he unconsciously set out to prove that the "I" "exists." Had he worked out the conception of cognition, he would have arrived at the true starting point for theory of knowledge, namely: the "I" posits cognition. Because Fichte is not clear as to what it is that determines the activity of the "I," he simply characterizes this activity as the positing of being, of existence. In doing so, he also limits the absolute activity of the "I." If the "I" is only unconditioned in its "positing of existence," everything else the "I" does must be conditioned. But then, all possible ways to pass from what is unconditioned to the conditioned are blocked. If the "I" is unconditioned only in the one direction described, it immediately ceases to be possible for the "I" to posit, through an absolute act, anything but its own being. This makes it necessary to indicate the basis on which all the other activities of the "I" depend. Fichte sought for this in vain, as we have already seen.

This is why he turned to the other of the two possibilities indicated for deducing the "I." As early as 1797, in his *First Introduction to the Science of Knowledge,* he recommends self-observation as the right method for attaining knowledge of the essential being of the "I": "Attend to yourself: turn your attention away from everything that surrounds you and toward your inner life; this is the demand that philosophy makes on its disciple. Our concern is not with anything that lies outside, but only with yourself."[34] To introduce the science of knowledge in this way is indeed a great advance on his earlier introduction. In self-observation the activity of the "I" actually seen, not one-sidedly turned in a particular

---

[34] *Sämtliche Werke (Complete Works) I,* p. 422.

direction, not as merely positing existence, but revealing many aspects of itself as it strives to grasp directly the world-content in thinking. Self-observation reveals the "I" engaged in the activity of building up the world picture by combining the given with concepts. For someone who has not elaborated the above considerations for himself, however, and who therefore does not know that the "I" only arrives at the full content of reality when it approaches the given with its thought-forms – for him the process of knowledge appears to consist of spinning the world out of the "I" itself. This is why Fichte sees the world-picture more and more as a construction of the "I." He emphasizes ever more strongly that it is essential for the science of knowledge to awaken the faculty for watching the "I" while it constructs the world. He who is able to do this appears to Fichte to be at a higher stage of knowledge than someone who can see only the construction, only the finished product. He who considers only the world of objects does not recognize that they have first been created by the "I." He who observes the "I" while it constructs, sees the foundation of the finished world-picture; he knows the means by which it has come into being, and it appears to him as the result of presuppositions which for him are given. Ordinary consciousness sees only what is posited [*was gesetzt ist*], what is in some way or other determined. It lacks insight into the antecedent, into the ground – that is, why something is posited in just the way it is, and not otherwise. To secure knowledge of these antecedents is, for Fichte, the task of a completely new sense organ. This he expresses most clearly in his *Introductory Lectures to the Science of Knowledge*, delivered at Berlin University in the autumn of 1813:

"This science presupposes a completely new inner sense organ, through which a new world is revealed which does not exist for the ordinary man at all." Or: "The world revealed by this new sense, and therefore also the sense itself, is so far clearly defined: it consists in seeing the premises on which is based the judgment that 'something *is*'; that is, seeing the foundation of existence which, just because it is the foundation, is in itself nothing else and cannot be defined.[35]

Here too, Fichte lacks clear insight into the content of the activity carried out by the "I." And he never attained this insight. That is why his science of knowledge could never become what he intended it to be: a philosophical foundation for science in general in the form of a theory of knowledge. Had he once recognized that the activity of the "I" can only be posited by the "I" itself, this insight would also have led him to see that the activity must likewise be determined by the "I" itself. This, however, can occur only by a content being given to the otherwise purely formal activity of the "I." As this content must be introduced by the "I" itself into its otherwise quite undetermined activity, the activity as such must also be determined by the "I" itself in accordance with the I's own nature. Otherwise its activity could not be posited by the "I," but at most by a "thing-in-itself" within the "I," whose instrument the "I" would be. Had Fichte attempted to discover how the "I" determines its own activity, he would have arrived at the concept of knowledge which is to be produced by the "I." Fichte's science of knowledge proves that even the acutest thinker cannot successfully contribute to any field of knowledge if he is unable to come to the right thought-form (category, idea) which, when supplemented by the given, constitutes reality. Such a thinker is like a person to whom wonderful melodies are played, but he does not hear them because he lacks an ear for music. Consciousness, as given, can be described only by someone who knows how to take possession of the "idea of consciousness."

Fichte once came very near the truth. In his *Introduction to the Science of Knowledge* (1797), he says that there are two theoretical

---

[35] *J. G. Fichtes nachgelassene Werke (J. G. Fichte's Posthumous Work)*, edited by I. H. Fichte, vol. I, Bonn 1834, p. 4 and p. 16.

systems: dogmatism — in which the "I" is determined by the objects; and idealism — in which the objects are determined by the "I." In his opinion both are possible world-views. Both are capable of being built up into a consistent system. But the adherents of dogmatism must renounce the independence of the "I" and make it dependent on the "thing-in-itself." For the adherents of idealism, the opposite is the case. Which of the two systems a philosopher is to choose, Fichte leaves completely to the preference of the individual. But if one wishes the "I" to retain its independence, then one will cease to believe in external things and devote oneself to *idealism*.

This line of thought fails to consider one thing, namely that the "I" cannot reach any choice or decision which has some real foundation if it does not presuppose something which enables it to do so. Everything determined by the "I" remains empty and without content if the "I" does not find something that is full of content and determined through and through, which then makes it possible for the "I" to determine the given and, in doing so, also enables it to choose between idealism and dogmatism. This something which is permeated with content through and through is, however, the world of thinking. And to determine the given by means of thinking is to cognize. No matter from what aspect Fichte is considered, we shall find that his line of thought gains power and life when we think of the activity of the "I," which he presents as gray and empty of content, as filled and organized by what we have called the process of cognition.

The fact that the "I" is freely able to become active in itself makes it possible for it to produce the category of cognition through self-determination; in the rest of the world, by objective necessity the categories are connected with the given corresponding to them. It must be the task of ethics and metaphysics to investigate the nature of this free self-determination on the basis of this theory of knowledge. These sciences will also have to investigate whether the "I" can objectify ideas other than those of cognition. That the objectification of the idea of cognition occurs through freedom, however, is already clear from the above discussion. For when the directly given and the thought-form belonging to it are united by the "I" in the process of cognition, the union of these two elements of reality – which otherwise would remain forever separated in consciousness – can only take place through a free act.

Our discussion sheds a completely new light on critical idealism. Anyone who has acquainted himself intimately with Fichte's system will know that it was a point of vital importance for this philosopher to uphold the principle that nothing from the external world can enter the "I," that nothing takes place in the "I" which is not originally postulated by the "I" itself. Yet it is beyond all doubt that no idealism can derive from the "I" that form of the world-content which is here described as the directly given. This form of the world-content can only be *given*; it can never be constructed out of thinking. One need only consider that if all colors were given us with the exception of one single shade, even then we could not begin to provide the shade from the "I" alone. We can form a picture of distant regions that we have never seen, provided we have once personally experienced, as given, the various elements needed to form the picture. Then, out of the single facts given us, we combine the picture according to given information. We should strive in vain to invent for ourselves even a single perceptual element that has never appeared within our sphere of the given. It is, however, one thing merely to be *aware* of the given world: it is quite another to recognize its essential nature. This latter, though intimately connected with the world-content, does not become clear to us unless we ourselves build up reality out of the given and the activity of thinking. The essential "what" of the given is posited by the "I" only through the "I" itself. The "I" would have no occasion to posit itself within the nature of something given did it not first find itself confronted by completely undetermined given. Therefore what is posited by the "I" as

166

the essence (*Wesen*) of the world is not posited without the "I" but through it.

The true shape is not the first in which reality comes before the "I," but the shape that the "I" gives it. That first shape, in fact, has no significance for the objective world; it is significant only as a basis for the process of cognition. It is the shape in which the world is first given, rather than a shape it attains through theorizing activity, that is subjective. If, like Volkelt and others, one wishes to call this given world "experience," then one will have to say: The world-picture which, owing to the constitution of our consciousness, appears to us in a subjective form as experience, is completed through knowledge to become what it really is.

Our epistemology supplies the foundation for true idealism in the real sense of the word. It establishes the conviction that in thinking the essence of the world is mediated. Through thinking alone the relationship between the details of the world-content become manifest, be it the relation of the sun to the stone it warms, or the relation of the "I" to the external world. In thinking alone the element is given which determines all things in their relations to one another.

An objection which Kantianism could still bring forward would be that the definition of the given described above holds good in the end only *for the "I."* To this I must reply that according to the view of the world outlined here, the division between "I" and external world, like all other divisions, is valid only within the given and from this it follows that the term "for the I" has no significance when things have been understood by thinking, because *thinking* unites all opposites. The "I" ceases to be seen as something separated from the external world when the world is permeated by thinking; it therefore no longer makes sense to speak of definitions as being valid for the "I" only.

VII.
CONCLUSION IN TERMS OF
THE THEORY OF KNOWLEDGE

We have established the theory of knowledge as the science of the meaning of all human knowledge. The theory of knowledge alone can explain to us the relationship which the contents of the various branches of knowledge have to the world. Combined with them it enables us to understand the world, to attain a worldview. We acquire positive insight through particular judgments; through the theory of knowledge we learn the value of this insight for reality. Because we have adhered strictly to this absolutely fundamental principle and have not evaluated any particular instances of knowledge in our discussion, we have transcended all one-sided worldviews. One-sidedness, as a rule, results from the fact that an inquiry approaches this or that object of cognition rather than the process of cognition itself. Our discussion has shown that neither the "thing-in-itself" of *dogmatism*, nor the "I" of *subjective idealism*, can be fundamental, for the mutual relationship of these must first be determined by thinking. One cannot derive either of these from the other – thinking must determine both according to the character and relation. *Skepticism* must relinquish its doubt of the possibility of knowledge, for there is no sense in doubting the "given," since it is untouched by all predicates. But should the skeptic doubt that *cognitive* activity could approach things, this can only be done through a thinking consideration, which contradicts the position. The attempt to ground doubt through thinking implies that thinking has the power to support conviction. Finally our theory of knowledge transcends both one-sided *empiricism* and one-sided *rationalism* by uniting them *on a higher level.* In this manner justice is done to both. *Empiricism* is justified by showing that as far as *content* is concerned, knowledge of the given is attained only by direct contact with the given. *Rationalism* also finds justification in this approach in that thinking is shown to be the *necessary* and *only* mediator of knowledge.

The worldview which has the closest affinity to the one presented here, built up on epistemological foundations, is that of A. E. Biedermann.[36] But to establish his standpoint, Biedermann uses concepts which do not belong in a theory of knowledge at all. He works with concepts such as existence, substance, space, time, etc., without having first investigated the process of cognition in itself. Instead of first establishing the fact that in the process of cognition, to begin with, two elements only are present, the given and thinking — he speaks of reality as *existing* in different forms.

For example, in § 15 he says: "Every content of consciousness contains two fundamental factors; *two kinds of existence* are given to us in it, and these opposites we designate as *physical* and *spiritual*, or as *bodily* and ideal." And in § 19: "What exists in space and time is material, but the foundation of all processes of existence, the subject of life, this also exists, but as an ideal; it has ideal being." Such considerations do not belong in a theory of knowledge, but in metaphysics, which in turn can be established only by means of a theory of knowledge. Admittedly, much of what Biedermann maintains is very similar to what I maintain, but the *methods* used to arrive at this are utterly different. No reason to draw any direct comparison has thus arisen. Biedermann seeks to attain an epistemological standpoint by means of a few metaphysical axioms. The attempt here is to acquire insight into reality by observing the process of cognition.

---

[36] *Christliche Dogmatik: Die erkenntnistheoretischen Untersuchungen im 1. Band (Christian Dogmatics: Epistemological Investigations in a First Volume).* An exhaustive criticism of this standpoint was delivered by Eduard von Hartmann; see his *Kritische Wanderungen durch die Philosophie der Gegenwart (Critical Wanderings through Contemporary Philosophy)*, p. 200 ff.

We believe that we have shown that all conflicts between world views result from the attempt to gain knowledge of something objective (thing, I, consciousness, etc.) without having first gained sufficient understanding of that which alone can elucidate all knowledge: *the nature of knowledge itself.*

VIII.   PRACTICAL CONCLUSION

The aim of the preceding discussion has been to throw light on the relationship between our cognizing personality and the objective world. What does the possession of knowledge and science mean for us? This was the question to which we sought the answer. Our discussion has shown that the most inward essence of the world lives in our knowledge. The lawful harmony that governs the cosmos comes to manifestation in human cognition. The human being is therefore called upon to bring into a realm of manifest reality those fundamental laws of the world which do indeed govern all existence, but which otherwise never come to existence. That is the nature of knowing: that in the world-ground, which is never to be found in objective reality, presents itself. Our knowing activity – expressed pictorially – is a continuous living into the ground of the world.

Such a conviction must also shed light on the way we take up practical life.

Our *moral ideals* determine the whole character of our conduct in life. Our moral ideals are ideas which we have of our task in life — in other words, the ideas we form of what we should bring about through our deeds.

Our action is part of the universal world-process. It is therefore also subject to the general laws of that world-process. Whenever something takes place in the universe we can distinguish a twofold character: the outer course of events follows in space and time, and the inner lawfulness.

To comprehend such a law in the spirit of human conduct is simply special instance of cognition. Thus the insight that we have gained concerning the nature cognition must be useful here as well. To know oneself as behaving a behaving personality means to know the law corresponding to one's behavior – that is, to possess the moral concepts

171

and ideals as knowledge. If we recognize these laws, then our actions are *our* doing. In such instances the law is not something given, lying outside the object in which the event appears, but is the content of the object itself engaged in living activity. The object in this case is our own "I." If the I has really penetrated its deed with full insight, in conformity with its nature, then it also feels itself to be master. As long as this is not the case, the laws ruling the deed confront us as something foreign, *they* rule *us*; what we do is done under the compulsion they exert over us. If they are transformed from being a foreign entity into the deed originating completely within our own I, all compulsion ceases. That which compelled us has become our own being. The laws no longer rule *over* us; *in* us they rule over the deed issuing from our I. To carry out a deed under the influence of a law external to the person who brings the deed to realization, is a deed done in unfreedom. To carry out a deed ruled by a law that lies within the one who brings it about, is a deed done in freedom. *To recognize the laws of one's deeds means to become conscious of one's own freedom.* Thus the process of cognition is the process of development towards freedom.

Not all our deeds have this character. Often we do not possess knowledge of the laws governing our deeds. Such deeds form a part of our activity which is unfree. In contrast, there is that other part where we make ourselves completely at one with the laws. This is the *free* sphere. Only insofar as man is able to live in *this* sphere, can he be called *moral*. To transform the first sphere of our activity into one that has the character of the second is the task of every individual's development, as well as the task of mankind as a whole.

The most important problem of all human thinking is: *to understand man as a free personality, whose very foundation is himself.*

ADDITIONAL NOTES

By Paul M. Allen

Kant*   Immanuel Kant, German philosopher, was born in Königsburg April 22, 1724. He entered the university there in 1740, enrolled for the study of mathematics and physics. His studies were interrupted by the death of his father, which left him in poverty. After he supported himself by tutoring for 9 years, the kindness of a friend enabled him to resume his studies, to graduate as a doctor and to qualify as a privatdocent. He occupied this position for 15 years. His lectures widened from physics to include much philosophy. Finally, after unsuccessful attempts, in 1770 he was given the chair of logic and metaphysics at Königsburg. In 1781 his *Kritik der reinen Vernunft*, Critique of Pure Reason appeared, and in 1783, his *Prolegomena*. After the appearance of the 2nd edition of the *Kritik* in 1787, Kant became famous everywhere in German intellectual circles, and his views were regarded as those of an oracle. From 1792-97 he was engaged in a struggle with the government concerning his religious views. In 1794 he withdrew from society, and gave up all teaching except for one public lecture course on logic. In 1797 Kant terminated a teaching activity that had extended over 42 years. He died in Königsburg on February 12, 1804 near the end of his 80th year. Little more than five feet tall, deformed in his right shoulder, his chest almost concave, Kant had a weak constitution. He never married, and followed an unchanging program of activities from youth to old age. For example, he never failed to rise at 5 o'clock, studied for 2 hours, lectured for 2 more, and spent the rest of the morning at his desk. He dined at a restaurant and spent the afternoon in conversation with friends. He then walked for about an hour — a walk which for years followed exactly the same course — studied for 2 hours more, and retired between 9 and 10. He was a prolific reader, especially in history, science, travel, and philosophy. He knew English history and literature intimately, especially in the period of Queen Anne. He read little of Goethe or Schiller, but often re-read Voltaire and Rousseau. He had little interest in nature, and in 80 years never traveled more than 40 miles from his native Königsburg. For further biographical details, works and translations, consult any standard encyclopedia.

Fichte*   Johann Gottlieb Fichte. Born in 1762, Fichte studied at Meissen, Pforta, Jena, and Leipzig with the intention of becoming a clergyman. After a teaching position in Switzerland, and enroute to another in Poland, he met Kant, under whose influence he wrote his *Study for a Critique of All Revelation.* The printer neglected to place his name on the title-page, and people thought the work had been written by Kant. When the true identity of the author became known, Fichte was hailed as a philosopher of outstanding merit. He lectured at Jena, Berlin and Erlangen. In 1807 he was made Rector of the University of Berlin. His death in 1814 occurred when he was at the height of his fame. Rudolf Steiner made extensive reference to Fichte, basing his doctoral thesis (published in enlarged form in the present volume), but perhaps his most memorable study of Fichte's life and thought was contained in a public lecture given in Berlin on December 16, 1915: *The Spirit of Fichte Present in Our Midst.*

Schelling*   Friedrich Wilhelm Joseph von Schelling (1775–1854). Often referred to as the Proteus among philosophers, Schelling was noted for his ever-changing alertness and brightness of mind and expression. Goethe had a very high regard for him, and spoke of him as "the most congenial philosopher I know." Schelling had a profound influence among the thinkers of his time, including philosophers of France and

England. His last years were dedicated to what he termed "positive philosophy," radically different from the philosophy of identity, the transcendental idealism, and the pantheistic tendencies of his earlier time. Rudolf Steiner made extensive reference to Schelling in his writings and lectures, on various occasions praising that philosopher's "important inspirations and suggestions for what must afterwards be said by Anthroposophy, directly out of spiritual vision, on many points of Christianity." Steiner further spoke of Schelling, "who really always made a significant impression whenever he appeared in public — the short, thick-set man, with the extremely impressive head, and eyes which even in extreme old age were sparkling with fire, for from his eyes there spoke the fire of Truth, the fire of Knowledge" (from a lecture given at Dornach, Switzerland, Sept. 16, 1924). Perhaps Steiner's greatest study of Schelling is to be found in his *Die Rätsel der Philosophie*, The Riddles of Philosophy, Vol. I, Ch. 7. For English translations of Schelling and further details on his life, see any standard encyclopedia.

Hegel*   Georg Wilhelm Friedrich Hegel [1770-1831], the great and profoundly influential German Idealist philosopher. The first long book he wrote, *The Phenomenology of the Spirit* (1807), remains his masterpiece.

Schopenhauer*   Arthur Schopenhauer (1788–1860), *Die Welt als Wille und Vorstellung* The World as Will and Representation, Four Books, publ. 1819 by Brockhaus, Leipzig. (English translation by Haldane & Kemp, 1883) Ref. Book I, par. 1, Ger. ed. Biographical data and translations of Schopenhauer's works, as well as extensive commentaries on his ideas have been published in English translation. Consult any standard encyclopedia for details. Rudolf Steiner edited a collected edition of the writings of Schopenhauer, 12 vols. with introduction by Steiner, publ. 1894.

Eduard von Hartmann*   Eduard von Hartmann, *Phänomenologie des sittlichen Bewusstseins*, Phenomenology of Moral Consciousness, German ed. p. 451. Born 1842, von Hartmann was originally an officer in the Prussian army. Because of an illness, he retired from military service and took up an intensive study of philosophy. In 1869 his *Philosophie des Unbewussten* (Philosophy of the Unconscious) appeared, and made him famous almost overnight. Of the many other works he wrote, this book remained his most famous. Rudolf Steiner describes a personal impression of von Hartmann, whom he visited in Berlin in 1888 following a philosophical correspondence with him over some years. This account may be found in Chapter IX of Steiner's autobiography. Steiner's present volume was dedicated to von Hartmann. The latter died in 1906.

*The Philosophy of Freedom**   CW 4; *The Philosophy of Freedom: The Basis for a Modern World Conception: Some results of introspective observation following the methods of Natural Science*, trans. Michael Wilson (London: Rudolf Steiner Press, 1964). (Alternative English translations are available under the titles *The Philosophy of Spiritual Activity* and *Intuitive Thinking as a Spiritual Path*.) Although Steiner did not identify it explicitly as such, CW 4 has come to be viewed as one of the four "basic books" of anthroposophy.

Karl Julius Schroer*   Karl Julius Schröer was born in Pressburg in 1825. In 1867 he was made professor of Literature in the Technical College of Vienna. In addition to his lectures on the history of German poetry as such, he lectured on Goethe and Schiller, on Walther von der Vogelweide, on German Grammar and Speech, etc. Rudolf Steiner was a pupil of Schröer, and refers to him in detail in his autobiography and in lectures. It was Schröer who recommended Steiner to Prof. Kürschner for the position of editor of Goethe's natural scientific writings. Schröer died in Vienna in 1900, and Rudolf Steiner has left an unforgettable word

176

portrait and estimate of him in his *Vom Menschenrätsel*, Riddles of Man, publ. Berlin, 1916.

the Specht family*   From July 1884 to September 1890, Rudolf Steiner was active as tutor in the home of Ladislaus (1834–1905) and Pauline (1846–1916) Specht at Kolingasse 19, Vienna IX. He taught their four sons, Richard, Arthur, Otto, and Ernst. Richard Specht (1870–1932) became a well-known author of many works including biographical studies of Gustav Mahler, Richard Strauss, Franz Werfel, Brahms, and Beethoven. Steiner gives details of this pedagogical activity in his autobiography, Chapter VI.

Rosa Mayreder*   Rosa Mayreder (1858–1938), Austrian writer, also known as a painter. Her entire life was passed in Vienna and surroundings. She was the author of a number of popular novels. In addition, she was active in the movement for woman suffrage in Austria, at one time sharing in the direction of the movement itself, and editing its periodical. She wrote the libretto for Hugo Wolf's only opera, *Der Corregidor* (1896). Rudolf Steiner refers to Rosa Mayreder in his autobiograph, Chapter IX.

*Goethe's Theory of Knowledge**   CW 2; *Goethe's Theory of Knowledge: An Outline of the Epistemology of His Worldview* (Great Barrington, MA: SteinerBooks, 2008).

Raymond Lull's *Ars Magna**   Raimon Lull (Raymond Lully), (0.1235–1315) Catalan author, mystic and missionary. Born Majorca. In 1266 a series of visions led to a marked change in his life and purpose. Spent 9 years studying Arabic in order to refute the heretical teachings current in his time. At Ronda he wrote his famous *Ars Major* and *Ars Generalis*. He made many journeys in France, Italy, North Africa in a burning crusade against the teachings of Mohammedanism. At Bougie, North Africa he was stoned outside the city walls and died on June 29, 1315.

the Biogenetic Law*   the teaching that living organisms come from other living organisms, as opposed to abiogenesis. The author of the modern formulation of "the fundamental law of biogenesis" was Fritz Müller (1864). Haeckel called Müller's formulation "the biogenetic fundamental law," which can be stated briefly as the teaching that in its development from the egg to adult stage, the animal tends to pass through a series of stages which recapitulate the stages through which its ancestry passed in the development of the species from a primitive form. In other words, the development of the individual is a condensed expression of the development of the race.

the laws of the mechanical equivalent of heat and of conservation of energy*
        The earliest statement of the law of mechanical theory of heat was formulated by the French physicist, Sadi Nicholas Lèonhard Carnot (1796-1832) in notes written about 1830, published by his brother in the latter's *Life of Sadi Carnot*, Paris, 1878. Further work in this direction was done by Ségun, Paris, 1839, by Julius Robert Mayer, c. 1842, and by J. P. Joule, who (1840-43) placed the mechanical theory of heat on a sound experimental basis.

Johann Gottlieb Fichte's philosophy of science* Rudolf Steiner's Inaugural Dissertation for his doctoral degree before the Faculty of Philosophy at the University of Rostock (Defense, beginning of May, 1891; Promotion, October 26, 1891) was titled *Die Grundfrage der Erkenntnistheorie mit besonderer Rücksicht auf Fichtes Wissenschaftslehre, usw.*, The Fundamentals of a Theory of Cognition with Special Reference to Fichte's Scientific Teaching. When the thesis was published in book form, as it appears here in English translation, a Foreword and one chapter were added to the original by Rudolf Steiner. These latter are included in the present translation.

Locke*   John Locke (1632–1704), English philosopher, scholar, chemist, student of meteorology, practicing physician, political advisor, traveler, and author. For details on his life and thought, consult any standard encyclopedia.

*Aenesidemus**   Gottlob Ernst Schulze (1761–1833), *Aenesidemus*, Helmstädt, 1792. A skeptical attack on Kant.

J. Müller*   Johannes Peter Müller, German physiologist and comparative anatomist, born in Coblentz, July 14, 1801. He studied at the University of Bonn, and was appointed to a professorship in physiology there in 1826. In 1843 he accepted the call to the chair of anatomy and physiology at Berlin University, which position he held with great honor until his death, April 28, 1858. He did much research in physiology, particularly in relation to human speech and hearing. His great work was the *Handbuch der Physiologie des Menschen*, 1833–40. (The English translation was made by Dr. William Baly, publ. London 1842). This work opened a new period in the study of physiology, and Müller is considered the main figure in the developments in this field in the mid-19th century. In his *Handbuch* Müller developed an entirely new principle which he called "the law of specific energy of sense substances." This he expressed as follows: "The kind of sensation following stimulation of a sensory nerve does not depend on the mode of stimulation, but upon the nature of the sense organ. Thus, light, pressure, or mechanical stimulation acting on the retina and optic nerve invariably produces luminous impressions." It is to this law that Steiner refers at this point.

Hume* David Hume (1711–1776), Scottish philosopher and historian. Albert Einstein wrote, "If one reads Hume's books, one is amazed that many sometimes highly esteemed philosophers after him have been able to write so much obscure stuff and even to find grateful readers for it. Hume has permanently influenced the development of the best philosophers who came after him." Among those influenced by Hume may be numbered Immanuel Kant, William James, George Santayana, and Bertrand Russell. Hume's writings and biographical and critical works concerning him and his ideas can be located by consulting any standard encyclopedia.

John Stuart Mill*   John Stewart Mill (1806-1873). A stern parent, James Mill taught his son Greek at the age of three, and at seven he studied Plato's dialogues. When he was eight he had to teach his sister Latin. His introduction to the utilitarian teachings of Bentham (the greatest happiness to the greatest number) at the age of fifteen was decisive for his life. His great work, *System of Logic*, 1843, is the analysis of inductive proof. He was a great champion of human rights, and in the second half of the i9th century his influence throughout Europe was very great. Today it is recognized that — to use Mill's description of Bentham — "He was not a great philosopher but a great reformer in philosophy." For details on Mill's life and thought, consult any standard encyclopedia.

Bibliography of Ronald H. Brady's Work

by Frederick Amrine

1. "Towards a Common Morphology for Aesthetics and Natural Science: A Study of Goethe's Empiricism," PhD dissertation, State University of New York at Buffalo, 1972, 327 pp.

2. *Toward a Man-centered Medical Science*, edited by Karl Ernst Schaefer, Herbert Hensel, and Ronald Brady, vol. 1 (Mt. Kisco, NY: Futura Publishing Co., 1977).

3. "Goethe's Natural Science: Some Non-Cartesian Meditations, " in *Toward a Man-Centered Medical Science*, vol. 1, edited by K. Schaefer et al. (Mt. Kisco, NY: Futura Publishing Co, 1977), pp. 137-66. †

4. *A New Image of Man in Medicine*, edited by Karl Ernst Schaefer, Herbert Hensel, Ronald Brady, Gunther Hildebrandt, Norman Macbeth, Uwe Stave, and Wolfgang Blankenburg (Mt. Kisco, NY: Futura Publishing Co., 1979).

5. "Natural Selection and the Criteria by Which a Theory is Judged," *Systematic Biology*, 28, No. 4 (1979), pp. 600-21. †

6. "Mind, Models and Cartesian Observers: A Note on Conceptual Problems," *Journal of Social and Biological Structures*, 4 (1981), pp. 277-86. †

7. "Dogma and Doubt," *Biological Journal of the Linnean Society,* 17, No. 1 (1982), pp. 79-96. †

8. "Theoretical Issues and 'Pattern Cladistics'," *Systematic Zoology,* 31, No. 3 (1982), pp. 286-91. †

9. "Parsimony, Hierarchy, and Biological Implications," in *Advances in Cladistics*, vol. 2, edited by N. I. Platnick and V. A. Funk. (New York: Columbia University Press, 1983), pp. 49-62. †

10. "The Causal Dimension of Goethe's Morphology," *Journal of Social and Biological Structures*, 7, No. 4 (1984), pp. 325-44.

11. "On the Independence of Systematics," *Cladistics* 1, No. 2 (1985), pp. 113-26. †

12. "Pattern Description, Process Explanation, and the History of Morphological Sciences," in *Interpreting the Hierarchy of Nature: From Systematic Patterns to Evolutionary Process Theories*, edited by Lance Grande and Olivier Rieppel (New York: Academic Press, 1985), pp. 7-31. †

13. "Form and Cause in Goethe's Morphology," in *Goethe and the Sciences: A Reappraisal*, edited by Frederick Amrine, Francis J. Zucker and Harvey Wheeler (Dordrecht, Holland: D. Reidel, 1987), pp. 257-300. †

14. "The Global Patterns of Life: New Empiricism in Biogeography," in *Gaia and Evolution: The Second WEC Symposium*, edited by Peter and Goldsmith Bunyard (Worthyvale Manor, Camelford, Cornwall: Wadebridge Ecological Centre, 1989). †

15. "Explanation, Description, and the Meaning of 'Transformation' in Taxonomic Evidence," in *Models in Phylogeny Reconstruction*, edited by Robert W. Scotland, Darrell J. Siebert and David M. Williams (Oxford: Clarendon Press, 1994), pp. 11-29. †

16. "Pattern Description, Process Explanation, and the History of Morphological Sciences," in *Interpreting the Hierarchy of Nature: From Systematic Patterns to Evolutionary Process Theories*, edited by L. Grand, and O. Rieppel (San Diego. California: Academic Press, 1994), pp. 7-31. †

17. "Cognition and Consciousness," in *Methodologies for the Study of Consciousness: A New Synthesis*, Proceedings of an International Symposium Held at the Fetzer Institute, Kalamazoo, Michigan September, 1996.

18.   "The Idea in Nature: Rereading Goethe's Organics," in *Goethe's Way of Science: A Phenomenology of Nature,* edited by D. Seamon and A. Zajonc (Albany, NY: SUNY Press, 1998), pp. 83-111.

19.   "Perception: Connections between Art and Science," presented as an invited paper at a conference sponsored by the British Museum of Natural History, London, April 4-7, 2000. †

20.   "Getting Rid of Metaphysics," *Elemente der Naturwissenschaft,* 2 (2001), pp. 61-78. †

21.   Chapters 1 ("Direct Experience"), 4 ("Intentionality"), and 8 ("Manifestation from Inside Out"), in Maier, Georg, Ronald Brady and Stephen Edelglass, *Being on Earth: Practice in Tending the Appearances* (Berlin: Logos Verlag, 2008). †

22.   "How We Make Sense of the World: A Study in Rudolf Steiner's Epistemological Work." Introduction to the present volume. †

† Available on the website of The Nature Institute, http://natureinstitute.org/txt/rb/index.htm

Printed in the USA
CPSIA information can be obtained
at www.ICGtesting.com
LVHW081544021223
765351LV00004B/216